Fluency
Through
Practice & Performance

Character Voices • Coaching • Repetition • Automaticity • Phrasing • Alliter

Reader's Theater • Dialogue • Oratory

Authors

Timothy Rasinski, Ph.D., and Lorraine Griffith, M.A.Ed.

Foreword by

Lori Oczkus

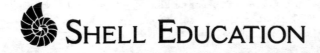
SHELL EDUCATION

Publishing Credits

Dona Herweck Rice, *Editor-in-Chief*; Lee Aucoin, *Creative Director*; Don Tran, *Print Production Manager;* Lori Kamola, M.S.Ed., *Editorial Director*; Hillary Wolfe, *Editor*; Robin Erickson, *Interior Layout Designer;* Corinne Burton, M.S.Ed., *Publisher*

Shell Education

5301 Oceanus Drive
Huntington Beach, CA 92649-1030
http://www.shelleducation.com
ISBN 978-1-4258-0262-2
©2011 Shell Educational Publishing, Inc.
Reprinted 2012

Table of Contents

Fluency workshops, programs, and books are plentiful since fluency made the list of five pillars of essential research-based instruction as identified by the National Reading Panel (2000) and the Reading First legislation. Yet, many of our students still lack comprehension and expression, pay minimal attention to punctuation and phrasing, and are unfortunately learning what the authors of this book call "fake fluency." *Fluency Through Practice & Performance* provides the critical next steps in cutting edge fluency instruction that will ensure reading success for our students. Tim Rasinski, a name synonymous with fluency, and Lorraine Griffith, an experienced classroom teacher, outline common sense fluency instruction that yields dramatic results. They describe what fluency is, dispel some misconceptions, and build a case for a rich practice and performance approach with dozens of convincing arguments for this super practical and student-centered method. Best of all, you just need this book to get started! Even if you've read everything you can about fluency, try these ideas and share them with a colleague. This resource is your desktop reference that will ensure fluency success!

Fluency is strongly linked to improved comprehension during silent reading (Daane, et al. 2005; Pinnell, et al. 1995; Rasinski, Rikli, and Johnston 2009). The authors' multidimensional definition of fluency includes word decoding accuracy, automaticity, and prosodic or expressive reading. They propose instruction that is rich, natural, and for genuine purposes. Five minutes a day of reading practice that emphasizes speed (NASCAR reading, according to the authors) won't do the trick! Students who solely practice speed do not make the same gains as those who receive instruction in the other aspects of fluency, such as phrasing and expression. Struggling readers in Lorraine's classroom have made on average 2.9 years' growth in reading achievement in one year. This well-rounded fluency program engages students in meaningful practice and performance to achieve results.

There are so many new, fresh, and exciting ideas about fluency in this text! Here are some that I can't wait to share in the many schools I work in across the country:

- THE secret weapon is coaching. Learn dozens of powerful ways to coach students in groups, individually, and by modeling.
- The gradual release of responsibility model (Pearson and Gallagher 1983) is creatively applied to fluency, including ways to conduct modeling through think-alouds, guided practice, and independent practice.
- This book offers rich and purposeful practice ideas such as cumulative choral readings, lucky listeners, and paired reading, while supporting English language learners and struggling readers.
- New reader's theater suggestions that require little preparation are included.
- The year-long flexible plan shows how to scaffold instruction using songs, reader's theater, and poetry through detailed weekly and daily lesson plans. We can grab this resource and teach!
- Many simple, quick teacher-directed assessment ideas that measure all aspects of fluency are included.

Fluency impacts our daily lives. I find it ironic that as even I write this foreword, my own home buzzes with activity centered around fluency—from my high school senior reading lines from *Hamlet* with a "sarcastic" tone, to my sophomore memorizing a poem, to my sixth-grader practicing a fund-raiser presentation. Notice how meaningful reading fluency practice and performance boosts comprehension—you will see it everywhere!

Please join me in thanking Tim Rasinski and Lorraine Griffith for such a wonderful, practical, and timely resource to improve the fluency of our students!

Lori Oczkus
Literacy Consultant and Author

To all teachers of reading who view reading as an art and a science and are willing to take the risk to teach reading fluency in an artful manner—through authentic practice and performance aimed at making meaning.

Think of someone you know who is a fluent speaker or reader. What does that person do that makes him or her fluent? We think that fluent speakers and readers use their voices to enhance the meaning of what is being said or read. Fluent speakers and readers raise and lower the volume and pitch of their voices, speed up and slow down, pause at appropriate places, and emphasize particular words and phrases for the purpose of making the listening experience more satisfying and understandable for the listener. Fluency is integrally associated with comprehension or meaning.

The concept of reading fluency has had a checkered past. In the 19th century, oral fluency in reading (elocution) was considered a primary goal of reading instruction. Readers were taught to read with good enunciation, expression, and volume. However, by the beginning of the 20th century, fluency had begun to wane. Reading scholars viewed comprehension as the goal for reading, and by the middle of the 20th century, fluency had largely disappeared from the reading curriculum.

Research in the 1980s to the present, however, has rediscovered the link between reading fluency and comprehension. Readers who read with greater oral fluency tend to be readers who have better comprehension when reading silently. And so, with the report of the National Reading Panel (2000) and legislation such as *Reading First*, reading fluency once again appeared on the reading radar.

Although fluency has once again become a major player in reading education, the way that fluency has come to be defined and taught in many classrooms has become a great concern to us. Reading fluency is most commonly measured by reading speed—faster reading has become associated with more fluent reading. And so, reading fluency instruction has evolved into encouraging students to read faster and faster, often with little regard for meaning. We now see students practicing oral reading by trying to beat their previous day's reading rate. Reading fluency instruction has turned into something akin to a NASCAR race.

We are convinced that this is the wrong approach to fluency. Can you imagine an adult reader reading as fast as possible? Would you call such reading *fluent*? Fast maybe, but certainly not fluent, clearly not satisfying, and absolutely not meaningful. We fear that if this trend toward speed reading continues, we will have grown a generation of readers who may be able to read quickly, but who find very little satisfaction or meaning in reading.

It is against this backdrop that we have written this book. Reading fluency is only important to the extent that it connects to comprehension. Let's go back to that initial example of a fluent reader—someone who makes meaning with his or her voice while reading orally. Although such a reader could very likely read fast if he or she chose to do so, a truly fluent reader uses his or her voice to make or enhance meaning. This is most commonly found in performances for an audience—plays, poetry, speeches, jokes, teacher and parent read-alouds, etc. In many cases, the play, poem, speech, joke, or book had to be rehearsed or practiced repeatedly in order for the reader to develop his or her oral reading to the point where it could communicate the meaning of the passage adequately. That is essentially the approach to fluency and fluency instruction that we take in our own classroom and clinical experiences, and it is this approach that we wish to share with you in this book.

Fluency is embedded in the oral performance of a text. Readers demonstrate their fluency by the manner in which they are able to create meaning through their oral interpretation of the words of a passage. And, the meaningful oral performance is developed and perfected through practice. Hence, practice and performance are natural keys to teaching and developing

10

fluency in students. Additionally, meaningful practice followed by authentic performance is a naturally engaging and motivating activity that nearly every student can find satisfying and enjoyable. Moreover, through texts that are meant to be practiced and performed, teachers and students have alternative ways to learn about and appreciate language in its various forms and through various content areas such as social studies, science, art, or music.

We have learned about the power and potential of practice and performance through our own work with readers—from young to adult—and from readers who struggle to those who are advanced. In this book, we share with you our own journeys to fluency through practice and performance. We will examine with you why fluency is important for oral and silent reading proficiency. We share with you how we teach fluency through modeling fluent reading, guided practice in reading, coaching students to develop their fluency, and of course, showcasing students' fluency through performance. We will provide you with models of how to organize and manage your classroom for fluency instruction. We will also explore what texts and textual features lend themselves to practice and performance, as well as explore methods for assessing the various dimensions of fluency.

If you are looking to make an impact on your students' growth as readers, then you need to look at fluency. And, if you are interested in teaching reading fluency in authentic ways that have been proven effective and engaging for students, then you need to look at practice and performance. We think that this book will help you negotiate your way to developing fluency instruction that will lead to greater growth and greater enjoyment of reading.

Timothy and Lorraine

Chapter 1: Potential and Pitfalls in Fluency Instruction

Reading fluency, the ability to read the words on the printed page accurately and effortlessly—with appropriate and meaningful expression and phrasing—was largely a forgotten element of the reading curriculum during the second half of the 20th century. Reading scholars thought of fluency as nothing more than oral reading and, of course, everyone knows that most reading done today is silent reading. So why teach fluency if it is nothing more than good oral reading?

In fact, fluency is, in essence, a neglected goal of the reading program. Indeed, that is just what Dr. Richard Allington called fluency in his seminal article from *The Reading Teacher* (1983). But Allington also argued that even though fluency was being neglected, it should not be. He pointed to some early research that indicated that many struggling readers are not sufficiently fluent and that instruction in fluency not only tended to improve fluency, but it also improved other key aspects of reading, including reading comprehension.

It took nearly 20 years for fluency to appear back on the radar screen. Thanks to the review of research conducted by the National Reading Panel (2000), fluency was once again identified as a key element in effective reading instruction. In its review of the research, the Panel concluded that there was sufficient empirical evidence to indicate that instruction in fluency leads to improved reading in students, especially with readers who struggle in achieving their full literacy potential.

And so, when President George W. Bush initiated his *Reading First* plan for improving reading education in the United States, reading fluency was identified as a central and required part of any reading program that was to be part of *Reading First*.

Now, that may have been the end of the story and reading fluency would go on to play an illustrious role as a cornerstone in successful literacy efforts. Unfortunately, somewhere along the way, fluency got a bit off track. Teachers and reading scholars began to see reading fluency as a bit of an albatross. Indeed, when the International Reading Association's *"What's hot"* survey for 2009 was published (Cassidy and Cassidy 2009), fluency was identified by a group of noted literacy scholars as a topic that was hot but should NOT be!

What happened to fluency to give it such a bad name? We think that the problem with fluency began with the way it was being defined. Some research found that reading rate, a measure of effortless and automatic word recognition—one aspect of fluency—was highly correlated with reading comprehension. Students who were automatic in their word recognition could focus on meaning rather than on the laborious decoding of the words in the passage. Hence, comprehension improved. Students who were automatic in word recognition tended also to be faster readers. Automaticity improved both rate and comprehension (see Figure 1.1 below).

Figure 1.1 Automaticity Improves Rate and Comprehension

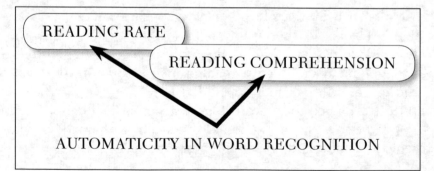

Somehow, over time, this model of reading fluency got twisted around. Automaticity disappeared from the picture and reading rate was viewed as the direct link to reading comprehension. Essentially, the model of reading fluency evolved into improving reading rate which, it was believed, would lead to improved comprehension (see Figure 1.2 on the following page).

Figure 1.2 Reading Rate Alone Improves Comprehension

Fluency became associated with reading rate; or, as some of our teacher friends have noted, fluency and reading turned into a NASCAR race. Students (and teachers) were given specific reading rate goals by school district administrators. They were informed that these goals should be achieved by the end of a school year. Well-meaning teachers designed lessons that were aimed primarily at improving reading speed.

We see this now in the reading clinic at Kent State University: when students are asked to read a passage aloud in order to assess their reading, they often ask the examiner if they should read the passage "as fast as I can."

Although we can see how this notion about fluency has evolved, it is simply wrong. We know of no compelling research that shows when students are taught to read faster they improve their reading comprehension or overall reading achievement. Indeed, we know of classrooms where teachers gave additional focus on reading rate; yet when those students took the state reading examination at the end of the year, they did worse than students in other classrooms in the same school where the fluency focus was not nearly so speed centered.

Still, this notion of reading fluency has found its way into our profession. Definitions of reading fluency more often than not include "reading quickly" or "reading words at a fast pace." Of course, many teachers and scholars know that reading fast is not fluency, and so there has been a backlash against fluency. Now we see that even though fluency may be a hot topic, if it is defined primarily as reading fast, then it shouldn't be "hot" (Cassidy and Cassidy 2009). Our biggest fear is that this wrong-headed notion about reading fluency will once again lead it back into the closet. Fluency will be taken off the radar screen, removed from reading curricula, exorcised from reading methods textbooks, and as a result, many children will remain struggling readers because fluency instruction will not have been provided to them.

Reconceptualizing Reading Fluency

We don't want fluency to go away. We know it is too important. We know that the lack of fluency may be a cause of reading problems for so many children. However, we do think that reading fluency needs to be reconceptualized. We need to go back to the roots of what it means to be fluent, whether we are describing a fluent speaker, a fluent reader, a fluent writer, or even a fluent driver, cook, or golfer.

We all know that fluency in reading, speaking, or anything else does not mean simply doing the task quickly. In the case of oral speech, we would all associate fluency with the ability to speak at an appropriate rate and with appropriate expression that reflects the meaning of the passage. Fluency is inexorably involved in doing a task well. A fluent speaker constructs meaning with his or her voice in such a way that a listener can take in the vocal input of the speaker and reconstruct that meaning. A fluent driver is not a fast driver. A fluent driver drives safely and efficiently to achieve the functional and meaningful goal of moving from one place to another. This may mean driving fast in some places of the trip, but also slowing down and even stopping at other places. It means signaling turns and lane changes. It means obeying the rules of the road—attending to those signs along the way that direct the driver of a car to stop, watch for children, get into the appropriate lane for turning, and driving at the indicated speed. Similarly, a fluent cook or chef is able to construct a satisfying meal in an accurate and efficient manner with the appropriate flourishes that define the dish as uniquely his or hers. You see that fluency is more than reading quickly; being *fluent* means the construction of something meaningful in an efficient but always functional way. Fluency is meaning.

We know that one of the best ways to become fluent at anything is through practice. One becomes fluent at writing by writing a lot. One becomes fluent at public speaking by speaking in public venues often. One becomes fluent at cooking through cooking often. How many of us have mothers who, when asked about a particular favorite recipe, have difficulty actually articulating the specific elements of the recipe? They have created that particular dish so often that it has become automatized—they know it "by heart." When asked to actually think through the specific ingredients and amounts, they have difficulty because they no longer process the recipe in a highly conscious step-by-step manner. The recipe has become internalized and can now be prepared in a fluent manner.

It is the same with driving. Do you recall how difficult it was to master the various controls, levers, knobs, and pedals when you first learned to drive? Driving was not an automatic task for you, and you weren't fluent at it. Yet, with practice—meaningful and motivated practice with the goal of getting your driver's license— you not only became accurate in your driving (you were able to go from here to there without bumping into anything, knocking into the curb, or scraping another car), you also became automatic in your driving. You are able to operate multiple controls at the same time, almost without thinking about operating them. Indeed, through lots and lots of practice, you are now probably so automatic or fluent in your driving that you can now operate this complex piece of machinery accurately and so fluently that it is possible to do other tasks while driving. You can converse with passengers, listen to the radio, think about what you are going to do in school today, and still drive with a high degree of accuracy. That's fluency. It allows us to perform meaningful tasks so efficiently or automatically that we are able to go beyond the basic task to a deeper, more meaningful level.

In reading, the same is true. We become fluent in reading by practicing. By reading *widely* (lots of different texts) and *deeply* (reading one text repeatedly or more than once), we develop not just accuracy but also efficiency or automaticity in our basic word decoding skills. When word decoding becomes automatized, we are able to turn our attention from decoding to comprehension—deriving meaning from the written text. When word decoding is automatized, we are able to consider other aspects of reading—attend to punctuation, read with appropriate expression, and give emphasis to different portions of the text to take meaning to a deeper level. In other words, practice creates automatization of word recognition, which allows for the reader to comprehend a text at various levels—literal, inferential, and critical interpretations.

Moreover, practice in reading means rereading a text to get to deeper levels of meaning. This deeper, or repeated, reading is especially important for struggling readers, students who find learning to read difficult.

But how can we make wide and deep reading an authentic and genuine task in our classrooms? In so many current programs, fluency instruction is given primarily through repeated reading. However, the repeated reading is aimed at having students read faster. Students practice a passage until they can read it at a predefined reading rate. Once the rate is achieved, students move on to the next passage and repeatedly read it until a desired rate is achieved. This is how reading and fluency instruction has become a "need for speed." And of course, the end result is fast readers who lack expression, pay minimal attention to punctuation and phrasing, and have little understanding of what they read. Not only are students learning what we call "fake fluency," they are getting little satisfaction or enjoyment out of reading fast. You can see why so many teachers and scholars in literacy are saying that fluency should not be "hot."

The purpose of our book is to oppose this disingenuous approach to fluency. We know that fluency is important and we want it to be taught in ways that are authentic, meaningful, engaging, and enjoyable for students and teachers. We think that the key to practice—especially deep practice, repeated practice, or rehearsal—is performance. We feel that when students know that they will have the opportunity to perform a text for an audience, they will have an authentic and motivating reason to practice.

That is the essential reason for writing this book: to explore with you the nature of teaching reading and reading fluency through practice aimed at an eventual performance. We know that this approach works because we have seen it work in classrooms and clinical settings around the country—our own classrooms as well as in the classrooms of teachers from kindergarten through high school who have wanted to make reading fluency a key part of their reading curriculum, and who also want to make reading fluency as authentic and engaging as possible. We invite you to join us on this journey. Perhaps it will bring back some fond memories of how you learned to read. Hopefully, it will give you inspiration and permission to try this approach to real fluency in your own classroom tomorrow. We begin our journey with an examination of the nature of reading fluency.

Points to Ponder

1. Do you have students who tend to struggle in reading? How would you describe those students? Are they good decoders? Do they read at an appropriate pace that marks their automaticity in word recognition? Do they read with appropriate expression? Do they have a good understanding of what it is they read?

2. To what extent do you think that students' difficulties in decoding, automaticity, or expression have a negative impact on comprehension?

3. If you have experienced or observed the approach to fluency instruction where students engage primarily in a quest to read fast, what have you observed that students are asked to do in that approach? How do students respond? Do they view reading fluency as an activity that involves comprehension? How might these students define reading and reading comprehension? How do the teachers involved in such an approach view reading fluency?

4. From your experience as a student and a teacher, do students enjoy reading for an audience, especially when they have had a chance to rehearse in advance of their reading? What kinds of materials do students tend to perform for an audience? How well do informational passages, the kinds of passages that are found in many fluency programs, lend themselves to performing for an audience? Why?

Tim and Lorraine Share Their Experiences

Tim Rasinski states:

"My own introduction to reading fluency came as a young teacher in an elementary school in Omaha, Nebraska. I moved from a classroom teacher to a reading specialist position where I worked with children in grades kindergarten through five who were experiencing difficulty in learning to read.

It quickly became apparent to me that I was into it well over my head. The nature and variety of reading difficulties was hard to fathom. I was especially perplexed by students who were clearly intelligent and creative, yet were experiencing severe difficulty in reading. How could it be that a child with an IQ of 120 or higher could be reading two grade levels below his or her placement? These children were certainly frustrated and discouraged, and so was I. I did not know what to do.

It was about this same time that I was working on my master's degree in special education/remedial reading from the University of Nebraska at Omaha. I began reading articles about reading fluency. In particular, I recall reading articles by S. Jay Samuels and Carol Chomsky, who wrote about making progress with children who had been making minimal progress in learning to read. Both described instructional methods that I had not considered previously, methods that focused on developing reading fluency.

Up to that time, I am not sure I had read or even heard much about reading fluency in my university courses or through professional development at my school. I recall looking through some of the textbooks I had used in my coursework and found reading fluency hardly mentioned at all.

And so, I began to employ and adapt the methods that Samuels and Chomsky wrote about—repeated and assisted readings—in my own work with students. I found that these methods did work remarkably well, especially with students who were experiencing difficulty in reading. And so, a good portion of my subsequent career in education has been to explore the nature of reading fluency and how instruction in fluency can be employed to help children, adolescents, and adults become better readers."

Lorraine Griffith states:

"As I think back to my introduction to reading fluency, my first thought is 'ugh!' I was visiting a college campus when one of the reading professors asked me, 'So how do YOU teach reading fluency in your classroom?' I couldn't begin to answer the question because I was not sure what reading fluency even was. But, I did know I was really frustrated with trying to teach struggling readers to comprehend grade-level text in a world of heightened testing pressure. I just didn't have the words in my teacher vocabulary to describe what I was hearing as my struggling readers read in the classroom.

My frustration was crystallized when I taught a child I'll call 'Alice.' Alice was reading at least two years below grade level. It did not take long to realize that she was struggling with decoding and comprehension.

She stumbled over many words in a text and made it a long painful process to trudge through a paragraph. So, when she arrived at the end of her journey through a short text, she had no idea how to answer those multiple choice comprehension questions at the end.

Early in the year, I made a plan with the reading specialist at my school: for 30 minutes each day, Alice would work on phonics in a one-on-one setting. Halfway through the year, the time would be divided between the continued phonics study and comprehension strategies. The teacher would read the passage aloud and Alice would answer the comprehension questions orally. Meanwhile, Alice was part of my regular classroom instruction with word work, comprehension strategies, silent reading, and teacher read-alouds. We were consistent throughout the year and finally arrived at the testing day. We could not wait to see Alice 'wildly succeed!' But she didn't. When it was time for the first break, Alice had not completed the reading of the first article and tears were running down her face. She had learned the decoding strategies without automaticity and had learned to comprehend a text while someone else modeled fluent reading. But she had not orally rehearsed the reading of a text because I didn't know the application of that missing link in reading instruction—reading fluency.

The summer following Alice's testing fiasco, I attended Tim Rasinski's 'Struggling Reader' workshop. When he began the reading fluency portion of his presentation, my ears perked up. He began talking about how fluency is best developed through practice, repeated readings of a given text, and that perhaps the best way to develop motivation to practice is to give students a chance to perform. He mentioned that certain kinds of texts lend themselves to performance—poetry, song, speeches, and reader's theater. He also gave proof that practice and performance using reader's theater worked by citing a study from San Antonio, Texas (Martinez, Roser, and Strecker 1999) in which primary grade students were given a weekly reader's theater script which they rehearsed (practiced) all week long under the coaching and guidance of their teacher. On Fridays, the students then performed their scripts for an audience of classmates and parents. On the following Monday, they began the routine once more with different scripts. Tim reported that the students using reader's theater made, on average, over a year's growth in reading achievement in three months! And they also made double the gain in their reading rate over a comparison group of students not performing reader's theater, even though there was no emphasis on reading fast when doing reader's theater. I was shocked by these results. How could such a simple intervention make such a dramatic impact on students' reading?

For years, I had heard about reader's theater but couldn't understand what all the buzz was about. I had used plays in my classroom and had not seen any amazing results except for a break in the weekly story routine. Challenged by the Martinez, Roser, and Strecker study (1999), I decided then and there to implement a simple routine of rehearsal and performance using reader's theater the following school year.

When the new school year began, I handed out reader's theater texts and told the kids to practice their marked parts each evening. On Friday, I gave small groups about 20 minutes to rehearse, and then they performed for each other. We clapped and shared encouraging comments. Reading fluency attention began to pervade most of our school day when text was involved. Kids began to notice when other kids read well. Or they would say, 'Let's go back and read that again with more expression.' This simple implementation worked miracles in my classroom. I saw the average gain of silent reading comprehension grow from 1.17 years in the three years before this implementation to 2.87 years in each of the three years following. My below-grade-level readers were making almost three-year gains in one year by simply entertaining each other! It was amazing.

So now, if someone asked me, 'So how do YOU teach reading fluency in your classroom?' I could respond with much more information than anticipated. A huge smile would spread across my face, and I would begin to tell about the revolution in my reading instruction."

This book is about reading fluency. Actually, it is more than that: it is about how reading fluency instruction can be made authentic and engaging for all students and continue to be effective in helping them become better readers. This is a nuts-and-bolts book that offers teachers the methods, materials, and ideas for actually making fluency instruction work in their own classrooms.

In this book, we take a particular approach to fluency. We feel that fluency can best be taught through a *practice and performance* perspective. Over the years, we have worked with children on a practice and performance approach to fluency, and we have seen the marvelous results that can be obtained. We have also developed classroom-based instructional materials that lend themselves to practice and performance. This book, then, is a guide for teachers who want to teach fluency through this authentic and engaging manner.

When students are given opportunities to perform texts that they have practiced for a real audience, they will have engaged in authentic fluency instruction; they will have engaged in text practice for the very same reasons that people outside of school engage in text practice. Fluency is no longer some mechanical skill that must be taught, measured, and tracked; rather, it is an organic and real part of the classroom life that is preparing children for activities in which they will likely be engaged when their school days come to an end.

But before we can jump into teaching fluency, we do need to spend some effort in actually defining the nature and scope of reading fluency.

Defining Reading Fluency

Perhaps the easiest way to begin our definition of fluency is to suggest that there are two essential components in reading. The first is dealing with text itself: readers must be able to decode the printed symbols on the pages. The second and more important aspect of reading is comprehension—turning the symbols not just into sounds, but into meaning.

Clearly, we all know that the most important component of reading is comprehension—making meaning. Fluency, on the other hand, deals largely with the first task, negotiating the printed page itself—decoding the words on the page, reading the words automatically, and reading the words with appropriate prosody or oral expression. Although fluency may not seem to be that important in the larger view of reading, in fact, it is essential to reading success. For readers to get to the point where they make meaning from printed text, they need to be able to break through the printed text itself—decode the words accurately, decode the words automatically or effortlessly, group the words into meaningful phrases and sentences, and read with meaningful expression.

Many readers who experience difficulty in comprehension have fluency difficulties that are at least one source of their reading comprehension difficulties (Duke, Pressley, and Hilden 2004). These are the students who, when listening to someone read, have no difficulty in making meaning. However, when they are asked to read the very same text on their own, they have difficulty in comprehension. They have difficulty making it through the print, and as a result, they have difficulty in making sense of the passage. Although fluency may not be comprehension, it is essential for comprehension to happen—even silent reading comprehension.

Components of Reading Fluency

We all think we know what fluent speech or oral reading sounds like—we know it when we hear it. However, fluency is not a unidimensional construct. There are at least three key components of reading fluency, and all three need to be addressed through instruction.

Word Decoding Accuracy

The first element in reading fluency is one that is often referred to as *phonics*. We prefer to call it *word decoding accuracy* or *word recognition*. Each term refers to the ability to sound or pronounce a word from its printed form. Phonics is just one way a reader may be able to sound a word, using the letter-sound relationships within the written word itself. There are other ways that a word may be decoded—from various patterns or groups of letters within a word; from the meaningful context that surrounds a word; sometimes by the shape, length, and overall configuration of a word; and probably most often, simply by sight or by recognizing a word as a whole unit instantly. We feel that the phrase *word decoding accuracy* better captures the notion of sounding words.

No matter what it is called, it is clear that word decoding accuracy is essential to reading success. A reader cannot read if he or she cannot decode the words. Difficulty decoding as few as 10 percent of the words in a passage can cause severe difficulties in reading comprehension.

The importance of word decoding accuracy suggests that it be taught directly to students. Students need to learn how to decode words, how they are spelled, and what they mean. A strong word study program is an essential part of any successful reading program.

The research of the last 50 years has failed to find one method of teaching word decoding that is best for all students. There are many ways to decode words, and there are many kinds of readers. We need to provide students with as many tools as possible to help them decode words. Although we do not endorse any one way of teaching word decoding accuracy, we absolutely feel that it needs to be taught directly to students. We do think that active engagement in game-like word study activities that students find enjoyable offers the most interesting possibilities for teaching word accuracy.

Word Decoding Automaticity

There are many things in life that we do automatically, without even thinking about it, or with only minimal attention: brushing our teeth, walking up a flight of stairs, tying our shoes, driving a car, etc. We know these are automatically done because we are able to successfully do other tasks while engaged in these tasks. For example, while driving a car, we can also converse with a passenger, listen to the radio, pay attention to landmarks, or think about today's lesson. The task of driving a car has become so automatized for us that we are able to divert at least some of our attention to other tasks.

For reading to be successful, word decoding needs to be automatized—so automatized that the reader can divert his or her attention from decoding the words in print to grouping the words into meaningful groups and making sense of the passage itself. Perhaps the best example of automaticity in word decoding comes from you—the person reading this book. It is very unlikely that you are having to stop at each word to sound it out. You are most likely pronouncing the words (even silently in your head) instantly, effortlessly, and automatically. The significance of your automaticity is that you are now using your cognitive resources to apprehend the meaning of what we are trying to convey through the words that we have put on the page.

Automaticity in reading is essential to reading success. Many of our students are accurate in their word decoding, but they are not *automatic*. They may be able to decode the words, but they have to stop at every third or fourth word to sound it out. Their reading is slow and labored as they try to sound out so many of the words. Not only is it slow, however, it is not comprehended as well as it should be. These readers are putting so much effort into decoding the words that they have very little cognitive energy remaining to construct meaning from the printed passage.

Because reading rate is an overt manifestation of automaticity or the lack of automaticity, it has been used as a means for assessing automaticity in reading. The research correlating reading rate with comprehension is quite significant and impressive. We feel that reading rate is a good indicator of automaticity, and automaticity is an essential contributor to reading comprehension. Thus, we use reading rate to measure our own students' automaticity.

However, we do not use reading rate as a main instructional goal of reading. (Recall the problem with fluency noted in Chapter 1.) That is, we do not work directly on making students read faster and faster. Here is where fluency instruction has gotten a bad name. Many well-meaning teachers, advised by their supervisors and some reading experts, make reading rate a major part of their reading curriculum. They prompt their students to read faster. They chart their students' reading rates from one week to the next and even have the students track their own progress from day to day. We feel this well-meaning but clearly inappropriate interpretation of fluency will eventually lead to a generation of readers who have learned to read fast, but do not understand what they read and get little enjoyment or satisfaction out of reading.

Reading rate may be an indicator of automaticity, but it is not the overt goal of reading fluency instruction. Comprehension should always be the goal. We suspect that everyone reading this book is a reasonably fast reader. How did you become fast as a reader? Did your teacher put you through the same exercises that students engage in nowadays that are aimed at reading at a certain rate? Did you perform one-minute reads on a daily basis, always trying to read faster than the day before? We suspect not. The way all of you who are reading this book became faster readers—or more precisely, automatic readers—was by reading often, orally and silently, from a variety of texts and text genres. We need to do the same with our own students. In this book, we will share with you simple classroom-based strategies and ideas for developing automaticity in ways that are authentic and engaging for students and teachers.

Prosodic or Expressive Reading

In Chapter 1, we compared fluency to automobile driving. A fluent driver drives so automatically that he or she can attend to multiple tasks while driving. In reading, automaticity allows the reader to attend to the meaning of the passage in addition to decoding the words in the passage accurately. However, we also noted that a fluent driver not only is automatic and efficient, a fluent driver knows when to slow down, when to stop, and when to speed up. A fluent driver knows to signal turns and lane changes and to be aware of other traffic on the road. In other words, a fluent driver is also aware of the rhythm of the traffic and the punctuation of the road. The equivalent to this in reading fluency is called *prosody* or *expressiveness*.

If you think about what makes someone a fluent speaker or reader, the word *expression* often comes up. A speaker or reader who uses his or her voice to convey meaning is considered *fluent*. Conversely, a person who speaks or reads without expression—in a flat, monotone, and staccato-like manner, with little enthusiasm in his or her voice—is often thought of as *disfluent*. A more technical name for expression, one used by linguists, is *prosody*. Prosody is the melodic part of oral language and includes tone, pitch, volume, phrasing, and pace. A person who employs prosody in reading is giving evidence that he or she is comprehending what is being read. To us, prosody is a critical part of fluency. It is the link between fluency and comprehension.

Word decoding accuracy and automaticity are clearly important in reading, but prosodic reading is where meaning and fluency meet. One can be accurate in word decoding and still not comprehend what is read. One can be automatic in word decoding, but if the reader does not use his or her freed-up cognitive resources to construct meaning, that reader is unlikely to comprehend what is read. If a reader uses prosody, however, there is a good likelihood that he or she is actively processing the text for meaning, and that meaning is manifested in the prosodic reading.

Researchers Peter Schreiber (1987, 1991; Schreiber and Read 1980) and Sarah Dowhower (1991) explain the importance of prosody in reading. They say that in reading, the reader needs to be able to chunk or phrase the text into meaningful units of multiple words—noun phrases, verb phrases, prepositional phrases, etc. In oral speech, phrasing is marked by prosody: the speaker uses his or her voice to help the listener know how to phrase his or her oral speech. In reading, phrases are not generally marked within the text. Punctuation does offer some help, but it is clearly an imperfect system. Schreiber argues that a reader needs to use his or her tacit knowledge of phrasing from oral language and apply it to phrasing written text. The application of prosodic knowledge from oral language is what allows this to happen in reading. So, when a reader reads with prosody, he or she is chunking or phrasing the text into meaningful units that allows comprehension to occur.

Research has demonstrated the relationship of prosody to reading comprehension (Daane, et al. 2005; Pinnell, et al. 1995; Rasinski, Rikli, and Johnston 2009). Studies of students from primary grades through middle school have shown that those students who read with good prosody in oral reading tend to have the best comprehension when reading silently. And with every drop in the quality of prosody in oral reading comes a corresponding drop in silent reading comprehension. Those students who read with the lowest levels of prosody tend to be those who read silently with the lowest levels of comprehension. Many of these students are those who are most at risk for reading failure.

The implication behind this research is that instruction in prosody, as well as decoding accuracy and automaticity, will lead to increases in reading comprehension in silent and oral reading and increases in overall reading achievement. Interestingly, although most programs for teaching fluency mention the importance of prosody and expression in reading, they seem to do so only in passing. We have found that most commercial programs for teaching reading fluency focus almost entirely on the decoding automaticity of fluency, with the greatest emphasis here on reading fast. Prosodic reading is treated almost as an afterthought.

We feel that ignoring prosody is an error in these programs. Prosody must be an equal partner in reading fluency instruction. Throughout this book, we will explain and demonstrate how prosody, along with word decoding accuracy and automaticity, can be taught to students in ways that are engaging and authentic, and that emphasize making meaning throughout.

Fluency has been called "the bridge from phonics or word recognition to comprehension." Indeed, we think that this is absolutely true. When we work on developing automaticity in word recognition, we are linking fluency to word recognition or phonics. We want readers to be so automatic in their word recognition that they are using most of their cognitive energy to make meaning out of the text and not on decoding the words. And when we work on developing prosody or expressiveness in reading, we are linking fluency to comprehension. For readers to read with appropriate phrasing and expression, they have to monitor the meaning of the passage. That's comprehension.

So, authentic teaching of fluency has very little to do with making students read faster. It has everything to do with improving reading comprehension and improving overall reading proficiency. In the following chapters, we explore how we can teach fluency in ways that are authentic, engaging, enjoyable, and effective.

Points to Ponder

1. Think about your own development as a reader. How did you develop accuracy, automaticity, and prosody in your reading? Were there specific activities or lessons that your teachers or parents engaged in with you to nurture these critical competencies?

2. Dr. S. Jay Samuels (1979) first described the importance of having students read a passage repeatedly. Recall instances in your own life when you read a passage (or for that matter, watched a television program, or sang a song) more than once. Why did you engage in the repeated reading, viewing, and/or singing? What implications might these memories have for your own teaching?

3. Prosody is usually associated with oral reading. However, for prosody to have a true impact on reading, it needs to be active during silent reading. Do you hear yourself when you read silently? Do you attend to punctuation, even when the punctuation is not marked, when reading silently? If you do hear yourself, how did this develop?

We know that fluency consists of accuracy and automaticity in word decoding, prosody or meaningful expression, and text phrasing in oral (and silent) reading. Now we need to explore how it can be taught to students—especially from a practice and performance perspective. We think that some very basic principles can guide you in making fluency instruction an integral part of your reading curriculum, from pre-kindergarten through the secondary grades.

Time

Time for instruction is always an issue. Time in the school day is precious; time given for one hour of the curriculum is time that cannot be used for any other area. In our opinion, 30–60 minutes per day need to be provided for fluency instruction in the elementary grades. Half that time should be devoted to decoding accuracy and half should be devoted to working on automaticity and prosody. If you tend to segment your reading curriculum into defined blocks of time (e.g., four blocks), one block needs to be devoted to decoding accuracy and one block to automaticity and prosody (see Figure 3.1 on the following page). We certainly recognize that this segmentation of time must be viewed as variable—on some days more time is devoted to one block over another. For example, on days in which students actually perform, more time needs to be devoted to automaticity and prosody.

It may seem that 30 minutes per day devoted to fluency should be obvious. Fluency is important, it has been identified by the National Reading Panel as critical to students' reading development, and it needs to be taught. Yet, in a recent evaluation study of reading instruction (Gamse et al. 2008) in the United States, it was found that, on average, less than five minutes per day was devoted to fluency! We can't help but wonder if part of the reason that reading achievement scores have not had the significant increases we might have hoped for—given the increase in government funding for reading (i.e., *Reading First*)—is because fluency continues to be a relatively neglected goal of the reading curriculum.

Figure 3.1 Example of a Block Literacy Curriculum

30 minutes: Word accuracy (word study)	**30 minutes:** Automaticity and prosody (fluency)
30 minutes: Guided reading (comprehension)	**30 minutes:** Written expression (writing)

Accuracy in Decoding—Word Study

Since fluency involves dealing with the printed word, instruction in word decoding is clearly called for. Before we can think of reading words automatically and with expression, students need to be able to read the words accurately. This calls for a dedicated block of time devoted to the study of words. We feel that word study is the foundation for later work on automaticity and prosody.

Word study involves all aspects of words: sounding words, spelling words, learning the meaning of words, discovering the history and origin of certain words, learning the nuanced or connotative meaning of words, as well as knowing the literal meaning of words, and so on.

There are many excellent books, resources, and methods on the market devoted to ways to teach words productively, such as *Daily Word Ladders* (Rasinski 2005) and *Making and Writing Words* (Rasinski and Heym 2007). Focusing on word families, word building, word sorting, word games, and high frequency words are all productive and engaging approaches to teach children about word decoding. Providing an in-depth treatment of word study is beyond the scope of this book on practice and performance. However, we will share with you how word study can be connected to the other parts of the fluency curriculum. Suffice it to say that the study of words is essential to success in fluency in particular and reading in general.

Gradual Release of Responsibility

Any learning—whether it is learning to read, learning math, learning a shot in basketball, or learning to drive a car—is optimized when a certain series of steps is followed. This approach is called the Gradual Release of Responsibility (Pearson and Gallagher 1983). In this approach, whatever is to be learned (or taught) is first modeled for the learner by the teacher. In essence, the teacher takes full responsibility for the task to be learned, and while demonstrating the task to the learner, the teacher engages the learner in a focused discussion in which critical elements of the task are highlighted (i.e., coaching).

As the learner begins to develop some understanding of the learning task, the teacher gradually shifts responsibility for the task to the learner. Initially, responsibility for the task is shared by both the teacher and learner; and little by little, the learner is given increasingly more responsibility until eventually the learning task is performed solely by the learner under the supervision of the teacher. Eventually, the learner will be able to perform the task alone, without the assistance or supervision of the teacher.

Hopefully, you should find this gradual release model intuitively appealing. Most successful, effective, and efficient task learning is imbued with this model. Learning fluency in reading is no exception. To become a fluent reader, the fluency task needs to first be modeled by the teacher, then shared in its performance by teacher and student, and finally performed by the students alone, under the supervision of the teacher. In the following sections you will see how the gradual release of responsibility is manifested in fluency instruction.

Automaticity and Prosody

Modeling Fluent Reading

As mentioned in the previous section, we subscribe to the instructional principle of learning through the gradual release of responsibility from the teacher to the student. That is, learning best occurs when whatever to be learned is first modeled by the teacher. Later, the teacher and student share responsibility in the learning task, and eventually, the student will perform the task on his or her own.

In the automaticity and prosody portion of fluency instruction, the teacher needs to model for students what automatic and prosodic oral reading sounds like. Simply put, this means reading to students the materials that eventually you expect them to read on their own. If you are unable to read to students, then you need to find another way to provide a model of fluent reading. This may mean getting another reader to model for students or providing a prerecorded model for them.

In addition to reading to students, the teacher needs to focus students' attention on the automatic and prosodic portions of the reading. You need to discuss with your students how you made meaning through your oral rendering of the text. Questions such as the following help draw students' attention to your own oral interpretation of the text:

- Did you notice how I slowed down and sped up my reading in these sections? Why do you think I did so?

- What did you think when I made this long pause at this point in the passage?

- I emphasized this particular word when reading. How did this affect the meaning of the passage?

Through this type of discussion, students see that you added to the meaning of the passage with your own voice. They know what to aim for in their own reading.

Sometimes we learn through negative examples. From time to time, you might want to read to students in a disfluent manner—excessively slow or fast, no expression, staccato-like in your delivery. Students will clearly see that such reading lacks meaning and enjoyment. They will quickly learn that although the words may have been read accurately, they have not been read fluently.

Assisted Reading

Going back to the earlier notion of a gradual release of responsibility, in developing automaticity and prosody in reading, we know that students need to practice a passage with greater automaticity and prosody with the help or assistance of the teacher. This is *assisted reading*. In essence, assisted reading involves reading a passage while simultaneously hearing it read by another voice in a fluent manner.

When one reads a text while simultaneously hearing it read in a fluent manner, word decoding and fluency improve, and the improvements in decoding and fluency lead to improvement in reading comprehension (Rasinski and Hoffman 2003). When a reader sees a word and hears a word orally, that word becomes locked in the reader's memory and eventually becomes a sight word.

Assisted reading can come in a variety of forms. The most common is choral reading where students read a common text orally at the same time. In choral reading, students are supported by their classmates and teacher who join in the reading. There are a variety of forms of choral reading, from whole-group choral reading, antiphonal choral reading (smaller groups that alternate parts), echo choral reading, and paired choral reading.

Paired choral reading, in which one developing reader reads chorally with a more advanced reader, can be a particularly powerful fluency tool. The intensity of the one-on-one focuses children's eyes and ears on the text. When students read and reread a text with a partner in this way, fluency and overall reading performance improve (Rasinski and Hoffman 2003).

Variations and adaptations of paired reading can be made to fit any reading situation. Keith Topping found paired reading to be an excellent parental involvement activity (2001). Parents and children are asked to read chorally a text chosen by the child with the child pointing to the text as it is read. When the child feels sufficiently confident and comfortable, he or she can arrange a signal with the parent to back off, essentially allowing the child to read on his or her own without support. Should the child begin to experience difficulty in reading alone, the parent can jump back in, adding his or her voice to the reading; this allows the child to continue reading without losing fluency or meaning. Topping's research found remarkably positive results when parents engaged in paired reading with their children for as little as 10 minutes per night (2001).

Assisted reading can also employ technology by prerecording the material on a computer, iPod®, or audio recorder. Then, the teacher arranges an instructional activity in which children listen to the recorded text while reading it at the same time. Research over three decades has supported and documented the use of recorded readings for assisted reading practice (Chomsky 1976; Carbo 1978a, 1978b; Pluck 1995).

Perhaps the easiest form of assisted reading comes when a teacher reads a text and has the students follow along silently. Again, as students track the text visually and hear it read to them by their teacher, the words in the text are more likely to find a permanent home in the head of the reader. No matter how it is done, assisted reading appears to hold great promise in helping students achieve accuracy and automaticity in their reading. When the assisted reading is in the form of an expressive and meaningful rendition of the text, we feel it is likely that students will also begin to emulate and acquire the prosodic reading patterns that are modeled through the assisted reading.

Repeated Reading

Automaticity in most human endeavors comes through practice. In reading, we often think of practice in terms of wide reading. Wide reading is the kind of reading that most of us do in our daily lives. We read a text, perhaps think about it or act on it, and then move on to another text—one reading after another. Wide reading is clearly an important part of learning to read. However, there is another kind of practice that we think is equally important in reading. We call it *repeated reading* or *rehearsal*.

Sometimes students read a text for a first time and they simply do not read it very well. Rather than ask them to move on to the next passage, sometimes we need to challenge them to practice that same piece, or a part of it, repeatedly until they are able to read it fluently. A strong body of research has found that when students engage in repeated reading, they predictably make improvements in word decoding, word automaticity, and prosody on the text they practice. More importantly, the same research has demonstrated that those gains transfer to texts never before practiced and that overall reading achievement improves (National Reading Panel 2000; Rasinski and Hoffman 2003; Therrien 2004).

During repeated reading, students are eventually asked to read a passage on their own several times until they are able to read it with appropriate levels of automaticity and prosody. Going back to the gradual release of responsibility model, repeated reading allows the student to eventually perform the fluency learning task alone, without the assistance but under the guidance of the teacher. It is highly predictable that with practice students will improve on the passage practiced. However, the key understanding about repeated reading is that when students move on to other passages, growth in fluency, word recognition, comprehension, motivation, and self-confidence as a reader will also be evident. When that happens, real learning is occurring!

Coaching

Teachers model fluent reading, students read while listening to a fluent model, and students practice on their own. All these are essential elements in becoming a fluent and proficient reader. However, to practice without feedback and monitoring may result in students simply practicing their own less-than-fluent reading. Students also need the assistance and feedback of an expert—the teacher. Without doubt, the most important element in all reading instruction is you, the teacher. In fluency instruction, the teacher takes on the role of a reading coach or director. He or she certainly models fluent reading, but the teacher also does what a good film director or acting coach does. The teacher is knowledgeable of good material for developing fluency, is able to find that material, and can match students to materials appropriate to their reading ability and interests. The teacher groups students with others who can work together to create a fluent rendering of a text. He or she listens to and observes students in their own reading, giving feedback and advice on how to improve their oral reading performance. The teacher monitors progress, makes plans, and alters instruction to meet the needs of students. He or she involves parents and others who can provide essential opportunities for students to continue their practice. And, of course, the teacher organizes opportunities for students to practice in class and eventually perform for an audience.

The teacher or fluency coach makes it happen. In the same way that an athletic coach guides his or her team to outstanding performances on the playing fields and courts, the reading fluency coach guides students to outstanding performances with texts, performances that are not only satisfying to students and the audience, but that will lead to higher levels of reading achievement beyond the scope of the passages that are practiced and performed.

Synergy—Putting All the Principles Together

The elements we describe may, by themselves, work to build fluency. Students who engage only in repeated readings or assisted readings will make gains in their fluency and overall reading proficiency.

However, when these and the other elements described previously in this chapter are combined or synthesized into an instructional sequence, they reinforce one another, and you end up with learning and reading achievement gains that are greater than if the instructional elements were presented separately to students. The whole truly becomes greater than the sum of the parts.

In this book, we present fluency instruction from a synergistic and holistic point of view. That is, we see fluency instruction—using practice and performance—as the key, fitting into an authentic and motivating instructional purpose (performance) that requires students and teachers to engage in modeling, assisted reading, repeated reading, coaching, and word study in which the obvious goal is the performance, but the underlying fluency goals include word decoding accuracy, word decoding automaticity, and prosodic reading.

Regular Instructional Routines

What we have described above are the essential elements of instruction aimed at improving that critical competency in reading—fluency. We need to keep in mind that these instructional ideas and roles are not a one-shot affair. They need to be delivered in a regular, consistent, and predictable routine.

Repeated readings or assisted readings done once every so often may be a nice diversion from the other instruction in a classroom. However, they will not deliver the results we would like or that our students need.

For repeated readings, assisted readings, and the other instructional elements to work, teachers and students need to engage in them regularly (we would recommend daily at a regular time of the day) in a consistent and synergistic routine that follows a gradual release of responsibility sequence. When this happens, students' reading success builds on itself and students will pull themselves up by the bootstraps to higher and higher levels of reading proficiency. Imagine a 30-minute daily routine for fluency instruction that follows these steps:

- **Monday:** The teacher models the reading of fluency passages two or three times while students follow along silently. Then the teacher prompts a discussion on the meaning of the passage and the qualities of the teacher's own reading.

- **Tuesday:** The teacher and students chorally read (assisted and repeated reading) the fluency passages together two or three times, using various forms of choral reading. Another discussion of how the passage was and could have been read ensues. Students are encouraged to practice the fluency passages under the guidance of their parents.

- **Wednesday:** The teacher divides the students into pairs and trios. Students continue to practice repeatedly (assisted reading and repeated) the fluency passages, coaching and encouraging one another as they read chorally, alternating lines, and reading alone for one another. The teacher moves from group to group coaching and encouraging students and eventually assigns specific parts for a Friday performance. Students are encouraged to practice the fluency passages with guidance from parents.

- **Thursday:** Dress rehearsal. Students perform their parts in a dress rehearsal for the Friday performance. The teacher again coaches students on their readings. Students are encouraged to continue practicing the fluency passages under the guidance of their parents.

- **Friday:** Grand Performance. Students perform their assigned parts for an audience of classmates, parents, and other school personnel. The positive feedback from the audience motivates students to continue practicing and performing for subsequent weeks.

- **Monday:** The routine begins again with new material assigned for fluency instruction.

The instructional routine that we just outlined for you is, in general, one that teachers around the country have used with remarkable success in improving students' reading fluency, word recognition, overall reading achievement, and motivation to read. You will notice in the five-day routine the various principles we have laid out in this chapter. As you go through this book and think of your own instructional setting and needs, think about how reading fluency and the various elements involved in nurturing can be made an integral and regular part of your reading curriculum for the entire year. The approach that we share with you in this book is intended as a regular instructional routine.

Oral and Silent Reading

Most people think of fluency as involving oral reading. This is true. However, we recognize that fluency is necessary for silent reading as well. Although most of the actual direct instruction in fluency involves oral reading, we also encourage students to engage in repeated and assisted silent reading. More importantly, research has demonstrated that practice in oral reading fluency yields results in silent-reading comprehension. Additionally, recent research in silent-reading fluency, in which students are given responsibility and held accountable for reading appropriately leveled materials, widely has also been found to produce positive results in students' oral-reading fluency and reading comprehension (Reutzel et al. 2008). Oral reading improves oral and silent reading; silent-reading fluency instruction also improves oral and silent reading.

So, as you work through this book in which most of the work we engage in with students involves oral reading, our overall purpose is to improve oral- *and* silent-reading fluency, oral- *and* silent-reading comprehension, and overall reading proficiency, both *silent and oral*. Additionally, we aim to improve motivation for reading, another important reading goal, through our practice and performance approach.

In the remainder of this book, we explore these various components of fluency instruction from the perspective of practice and performance. From our own experience and the experiences of other teachers, we will share with you ideas and approaches that will help you make fluency instruction work for you and your students.

Points to Ponder

1. Inventory your own teaching. Is reading fluency part of your reading curriculum? How many days per week do you devote to fluency? How much time per day do you devote to fluency? Is it enough? (Recall the recent study that showed that less than five minutes per day on average is given to fluency instruction.)

2. Think of instances in which you have used the gradual release of responsibility in your own teaching. How did using this approach impact your students' learning?

3. Do you read to your students daily? When you read, do you try to read with meaningful expression? Do you ever talk to your students about how you try to put expression into your voice for reading?

4. Does assisted reading occur in your own classroom? Describe regular occurrences of assisted reading in your reading curriculum.

5. Does repeated reading occur in your own classroom? Describe regular occurrences of repeated reading in your reading curriculum.

6. What are some literature pieces you can see worthy of your class's repeated reading? How could you tie those selections to the content areas or your writing block?

Lorraine Griffith states:

"Years ago, my childhood was filled with practice, and most notably practicing the piano. My mom started my sisters and me in piano lessons at the ripe old age of seven with the idea that we would continue through high school. The notion of 'let's just try this and see if you like it' was not part of my parents' child-rearing philosophy. My rural farm family was all about hard work. We didn't really question the 30 minutes required at the piano each day. So, I've had time to think about practice.

Some dictionary definitions of the word 'practice' are simply stated as being a repetition of a specific activity over and over. But that doesn't mean that the practice creates mastery of the desired skill. It takes hard work during the practice period with an authentic goal in mind. Normally, that goal is to become proficient enough at whatever is being practiced to eventually perform for an audience in a way in which the audience finds satisfaction and appreciates the performance. Now in piano, it was knowing the correct notes and fingering first of all. The tempo was addressed, but I was not asked to show mastery by playing fast, but by playing exactly as fast or as slow as the composer specified or as the style of the piece indicated. Then, we would move toward dynamics, loud and soft. As the practice of a musical piece continued, my teacher would expect me to anticipate phrasing and interpret sensitive nuances within each phrase. In college piano, I was asked to move out from the notes on the sheet music and create my own interpretations of basic melody lines, without deviating much from the composer's tune. My hard practice was eventually rewarded when I performed my work at recitals."

My years of work with piano are very similar to the coaching done in the classroom toward being a fluent reader. There are teachers who rely on the simple definition of fluency where the reading passage is read tediously over and over again for the superficial goal of increasing reading speed. Initially, the children demonstrate mastery by reading the words in the text correctly. Then, as their own child-like desire to interpret kicks in, the children seem to want to speed up and become loud, very loud! Unless a teacher intervenes with appropriate coaching aimed at reading for meaning, the students will end up practicing a very loud, fast, and well-pronounced text over and over and over again. And, they will stay on the same level of reading fluency and reading comprehension with each new text.

As a teacher of fluency, I have learned that the power of this instructional focus is in the rehearsal time. Profitable practice is repeating something over and over again, with new and authentic goals for each rehearsal—making our ultimate goal a meaningful interpretation of the text for an audience. So, when rehearsing any of the avenues to fluency in the following sections of this chapter, there is a routine to follow with the coaching, very similar to the routine I followed in piano lessons.

The first focus of reading a new passage in any style is to be sure each child can read the words accurately, enunciating each word and pronouncing each word correctly. The text needs to be read at a rate that is appropriate for the type of text—reading a thoughtful poem requires a different reading rate than reading a funny tongue twister. After the text is read with good diction and speed, the child needs to focus on interpreting the text with appropriate variations of intonation, with phrasing implied by the punctuation and with the musical quality of prosody. This last step of focusing on expression is when the child secures the deeper meaning and demonstrates the comprehension that has come with a deeper reading of the text.

Because each avenue to fluency is a bit different, you may want to cover these steps of coaching all in one teaching block or spread them out over a week or two. The order of applying the steps to fluent reading may vary with teachable moments. But, in each experience, you will be working toward the ultimate goal of reading so well that the comprehension is demonstrated by the quality of reading.

A Variety of Avenues

When I began focusing on reading fluency in my classroom, I thought I had to incorporate a reader's theater script every week or I wasn't really teaching fluency. I have since learned that there are many avenues to teaching fluency well. And because we all know students learn differently and come to us at different levels of coaching needs, we should feel free to vary instructional routines for practicing texts.

There are several different approaches for practicing and performing fluency in reading. Each methodology has advantages for certain types of learners. As students are informally assessed throughout the school year, you will become attuned to what the needs are of your class as a whole and in smaller groups. In my classroom, I vary these routines often based upon the needs I see in my students. They are presented in Figure 4.1 on the following page in an order from the most dependent reading, as in choral singing, to the most independent reading exhibited in songs.

Figure 4.1 Continuum of Practice and Performance

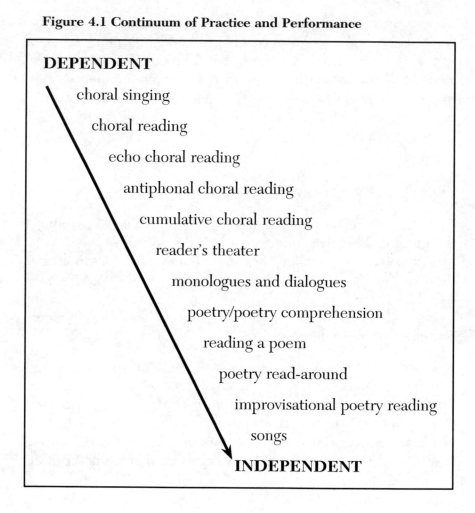

DEPENDENT

choral singing

choral reading

echo choral reading

antiphonal choral reading

cumulative choral reading

reader's theater

monologues and dialogues

poetry/poetry comprehension

reading a poem

poetry read-around

improvisational poetry reading

songs

INDEPENDENT

Choral Singing

Most of us have memories of singing throughout our school life. Many of us spent hours lying on the floor singing along with the lyrics on album sleeves or CD inserts of some of our favorite recording artists in middle and high school. Now we know that all those hours spent with song lyrics, when our parents thought we should be studying, may have been beneficial to our reading fluency. In the past few years, there has been growing evidence of the value of using choral singing in classrooms.

Choral singing involves the singing and/or oral reading of the lyrics of a song or text with other voices that support one another. Those other voices can be classmates, teachers, family members, or anyone else who joins in the chorus.

The procedure for teaching fluency through song is simple. The text is displayed for all of the students to follow, and then we sing. Recordings are helpful for teachers who do not feel comfortable leading the group with their own voices. Because the tempo requires movement through text and the meaning is already built into a musical phrase, choral singing is very helpful with struggling readers and English language learners. Students are also learning vocabulary appropriate to the theme or topic of the song. For example, if students are singing their national anthem or other patriotic songs either from their country or from other countries, they are learning a set of patriotic vocabulary. But they aren't just learning the words in a vocabulary list; they are learning the words in context with rich meaning and adding to their cultural knowledge by being able to sing along at a patriotic celebration.

Consider the lyrics for the American song "Hail to the Chief" (Gamse 1810):

"Hail to the Chief"
by Albert Gamse

Hail to the Chief we have chosen for the nation.
Hail to the Chief! We salute him, one and all.
Hail to the Chief, as we pledge cooperation
In proud fulfillment of a great, noble call.
Yours is the aim to make this grand country grander.
This you will do, that's our strong, firm belief.
Hail to the one we selected as commander.
Hail to the President! Hail to the Chief!

If you and your students are looking for words and phrases that make up a definition of *president* or *presidency*, it is all here: *chosen for the nation, salute, great noble call, commander,* and *chief.* And these words are written with respect embedded in the words and in the strong rhythm and melody.

Choral Reading

In choral reading, students simply read a text together in unison. Unison reading is obviously empowering for students who struggle with decoding and with recognizing vocabulary words. As the text is repeated several times, the stumbling, struggling reader becomes a confident surface reader of text who is ready to delve deeper into comprehension.

The additional focus in this reading style draws students into that deeper understanding by attending to the punctuation and phrasing closely and reading more and more expressively with each repeated read.

Although choral reading appears at the outset to be easy, it can become very unmanageable if a few loud students drag the text and forget to focus on expressive phrasing. I tell my students our goal is to read with grace, like gazelles, instead of marching through the text like elephants. As students read poetry chorally, they need to be learning to read a poem in the tone intended by the author. Consider the serious tone of "In Flanders Field," written by Canadian poet John McCrae (1915) on the following page, contrasted with a much lighter and even silly air in "Father William" (page 56) written by Lewis Carroll (1865).

"In Flanders Fields"
by Lieutenant Colonel John McCrae, MD

In Flanders Fields the poppies blow
Between the crosses row on row,
That mark our place; and in the sky

The larks, still bravely singing, fly
Scarce heard amid the guns below.

We are the Dead. Short days ago
We lived, felt dawn, saw sunset glow,
Loved and were loved, and now we lie
In Flanders fields.

Take up our quarrel with the foe:
To you from failing hands we throw
The torch; be yours to hold it high.
If ye break faith with us who die
We shall not sleep, though poppies grow
In Flanders fields.

"Father William"
by Lewis Carroll

"You are old, Father William," the young man said,
"And your hair has become very white;
And yet you incessantly stand on your head—
Do you think, at your age, it is right?"

"In my youth," Father William replied to his son,
"I feared it would injure the brain;
But now that I'm perfectly sure I have none,
Why, I do it again and again."

"You are old," said the youth, "as I mentioned before,
And have grown most uncommonly fat;
Yet you turned a back-somersault in at the door—
Pray, what is the reason of that?"

"In my youth," said the sage, as he shook his grey locks,
"I kept all my limbs very supple
By the use of this ointment—one shilling the box—
Allow me to sell you a couple."

"You are old," said the youth, "and your jaws are too weak
For anything tougher than suet;
Yet you finished the goose, with the bones and the beak—
Pray, how did you manage to do it?"

"In my youth," said his father, "I took to the law,
And argued each case with my wife;
And the muscular strength, which it gave to my jaw,
Has lasted the rest of my life."

"You are old," said the youth; "one would hardly suppose
That your eye was as steady as ever;
Yet you balanced an eel on the end of your nose—
What made you so awfully clever?"

"I have answered three questions, and that is enough,"
Said his father; "don't give yourself airs!
Do you think I can listen all day to such stuff?
Be off, or I'll kick you down stairs!"

Echo Choral Reading

The echo choral reading technique is very helpful for struggling readers and English language learners. Students may require some help with the word pronunciations, phrasing, and expression in a poem or prose reading. Echo choral reading can be effective in these situations.

Choral reading often becomes bogged down with "elephants"—students who read in a heavy, loud, laborious manner. But when students echo your modeled reading, you can show what you want the students to do in phrasing and expression. Imagine this to be a choir rehearsal where the director wants to work phrase-by-phrase or line-by-line with musical reading. A student needs to hear your voice rise and fall with the text before he or she will begin to understand what you mean by "read expressively."

Because understanding poetry is about seeing the chunks of text that make meaning, students will understand the text more deeply as they hear you shape the phrases and then imitate your variations of voice. Echo choral reading allows students to work on these different skills as you model.

Seeing the intended meaning in poetry is very difficult for some of our students. Consider the following passage from *Texts for Fluency Practice*, Grades 2–3 (Rasinski 2007) titled "Way Down South":

"Way Down South"
Anonymous

Way down South where bananas grow,
A little ant stepped on an elephant's toe,
The elephant cried with tears in his eyes,
'Why don't you pick on someone your size?'

By using appropriate voicing for the storyteller and then a contrasting teary, whiny voice for the elephant, the poem will come alive to the children. They will see the humor in it. The verses that follow will become entertaining to them more easily, when the voicing is modeled and the text is interpreted.

Antiphonal Choral Reading

In antiphonal choral readings, the text is divided into multiple sections for two or more groups of readers. Similar to whole-group choral reading, students still must be coached to read with the interpretation of text being the most important focus of the reading. One of the reasons I love the antiphonal choral reading is because it is like reader's theater with training wheels. After the students are comfortable reading in choral groups, you can reduce the size of the groups until they are actually performing as a duet or trio, one student for each part.

Consider the earlier reference to "Father William" by Lewis Carroll (1898). By simply assigning half the class to be Father William and the other half of the class to be the young person, you have a wonderful antiphonal piece. As the students gain confidence in reading in a large group, the groups can become smaller and smaller until there are only two characters reading the text.

When thinking about the younger crowd, there are many poems and jingles that are written inviting children to read antiphonally. For example, let's look at the familiar nursery rhyme "One, Two, Buckle My Shoe" (1805):

"One, Two, Buckle My Shoe"
Anonymous

One, two,
Buckle my shoe.
Three, four,
Shut the door.

Five, six,
Pick up sticks.
Seven, eight,
Lay them straight.
Nine, ten,
Do it again.

These simple poems are easily arranged for two groups of students. Groups can take turns reading the first and second lines alternately. This simple poem not only teaches the obvious rhyming pattern but it also teaches about voices. Students may be asked to read the lines in different ways...sweetly, angrily, impatiently, or happily. By reading in an antiphonal way, all of the students will be practicing the interpretation of text in a very comfortable and secure setting.

One of the favorite antiphonal readings in my class each year is an arrangement written with my class one spring as we were studying symbiotic animals and animals who compete for prey. The symbiotic animals were characterized as loving, hugging creatures; and the competitive animals were raging, killing machines. The vocabulary took on life as the students divided into two groups to practice fluent reading as oppositely personified members of the food chain.

"Symbiosis and Competition"
by Mrs. Griffith's 2006–2007 fifth-grade class

All: *We are living organisms.*
          We are the food chain.

Group 1: *We are symbiotic.*

Group 2: *We are competitive.*

Group 1: *We are into long-term relationships because we need one another.*

Group 2: *We are into contests because resources are limited.*

Group 1: *We will hug you.*

Group 2: *We will rip you apart.*

Group 1: *We love each other.*

Group 2: *We hate each other.*

Group 1: *We want peace.*

Group 2:   We want war.

Group 1:   We are the cleaner fish and the sharks living in harmony.

Group 2:   We are the cheetahs and the hyenas tracking the same zebra.

Group 1:   We are the honeybees and the orange blossoms.

Group 2:   We are the owls and the hawks poised to pounce on a mouse.

Group 1:   Like magnet and steel.

Group 2:   Like oil and water.

Group 1:   Living together.

Group 2:   Living apart.

Group 1:   A mutual benefit.

Group 2:   A winner and a loser.

Group 1:   We are symbiotic.

Group 2:   We are competitive.

All: We are living organisms.
            We are the food chain.

Cumulative Choral Reading

You may find cumulative choral readings to be one of your students' favorite ways to read a poem or speech. This is a technique that is wonderful for teaching timing and phrasing. When using a poem, one reader begins with a phrase or line and continues to read the entire poem as other readers are added with each new phrase or line. By the end of the text, all of the students are reading. Using this fluency technique at the end of a cumulative choral reading, perhaps using the most famous lines of a speech, demonstrates the mounting energy intended when the speaker delivered the original speech. Consider these lines from Winston Churchill's "Blood, Sweat, and Tears" speech (1940):

"Blood, Sweat, and Tears"
by Winston Churchill

Group 1:	You ask, what is our aim? I can answer in one word. It is victory.
Groups 1–2:	Victory at all costs—
Groups 1–3:	Victory in spite of all terrors—
Groups 1–4:	Victory, however long and hard the road may be,
All:	…for without victory there is no survival.

By adding voices for each line, there is a mounting energy that focuses on the text's rich meaning and allows students to sense the building intensity of those powerful words.

Reverse cumulative choral reading works in the opposite direction as cumulative choral reading. In reverse cumulative choral reading, the entire group of readers begin reading. Then, at the end of each line or other appropriate segment of the text, one or more readers peels away until the final line or text segment is read by only one or a few readers. In reverse cumulative reading, you begin with many readers but end with only a few. This form of choral reading works best with poems or other texts that you want to start in a large voice but end in a whisper.

Reader's Theater

Reader's theater is used when students are ready to perform as individual readers. Each student is assigned a part in a script to be read aloud. The script is handed out to students with the parts marked for them to study, rehearse, interpret, and perform when they are ready. The advantage of using reader's theater is for the individual student to find his or her own voice as a reader and to demonstrate the comprehension of text with using only the human voice—no memorization, no props, no costumes, and no scene changes. Obviously, this fluency form is moving toward the more personal and is risky for students. And, it is still my favorite!

During my second year of teaching reading fluency in fourth grade, I had the privilege of teaching a very bright but painfully shy girl named Elizabeth. We were beginning a unit on North Carolina during the Civil Rights period of history. I chose a reader's theater script, "The Sojourner Truth Story" (Isecke 2009), and asked Elizabeth to play the lead character. As usual, I marked the part and sent Elizabeth home to study it. Her mother saw it in her homework folder and loved the script. She and Elizabeth talked about the period of history and what it was like for African American women during that period of history. Karen, Elizabeth's mom, then did something amazing! She sent Elizabeth out to the field near their house and told her to practice the part of Sojourner Truth until Karen could hear her back at the house. And that was the day that Elizabeth found her voice. At the end of the performance, it was an incredible moment when Elizabeth, as Sojourner, shouted, "And ain't I a woman?"

Assigned to that same script was a boy named Gabe who had always been placed in the lowest reading group. He stuttered and was very nervous to have the part in this harder script. He worked and worked on his part. He didn't have the advantage of a parent who sent him out to a field, so we worked in class. On performance day, the students in his group were patient when he had trouble beginning; one of the girls said the lines with him until he got going. But, once he had his reading motor revved up, he flew through his part beautifully and articulately because of his repeated practice.

On that day, my students were performing as soloists, but it was like one moving unit of passionate speech. I fought tears as Sojourner Truth's voice rang out and I knew the kids all heard it!

"Ain't I a Woman?"
by Sojourner Truth

[...] That man over there says that women need to be helped into carriages, and lifted over ditches, and to have the best place everywhere. Nobody ever helps me into carriages, or over mud-puddles, or gives me any best place! And ain't I a woman? Look at me! Look at my arm! I have ploughed and planted, and gathered into barns, and no man could head me! And ain't I a woman? I could work as much and eat as much as a man—when I could get it—and bear the lash as well! And ain't I a woman? I have borne thirteen children, and seen most all sold off to slavery, and when I cried out with my mother's grief, none but Jesus heard me! And ain't I a woman? [...]

Then they talk about this thing in the head; what's this they call it? "Intellect." That's it. What's that got to do with women's rights or Negroes' rights? If my cup won't hold but a pint, and yours holds a quart, wouldn't you be mean not to let me have my little half measure full?

If the first woman God ever made was strong enough to turn the world upside down all alone, these women together ought to be able to turn it back, and get it right side up again! And now they is asking to do it, the men better let them.

Obliged to you for hearing me, and now old Sojourner ain't got nothing more to say.

Monologues and Dialogues

This section began with a chorus and now wraps up with a duet and a solo. Monologues are the solos in reading fluency. One of the easiest ways to collect monologues is to have students find their own passages in books written in the first person. The *Dear America* series (Scholastic 1996–2004) is a great example of books written from one viewpoint because of the journal structure of the fictional writing. Obviously, dramatic reading from any journals of historical figures will render great fodder for solo reading. By reading various dramatic passages from these books, you are serving two purposes: dramatically interpreting a text with one voice and advertising the book to be read by the rest of the class.

Dialogues are essentially conversations performed by two voices (for our purposes we count the performance of a conversation or exchange of letters or notes between two, three, or more performers as *dialogues*). Factual or fictional dialogues work remarkably well for practice and performance. Many books are written with strong dialogues that students can easily turn into practice and performance (e.g., Arnold Lobel's *Frog and Toad* series, 1970–1979).

Other dialogues can be found in history or written by students themselves. Imagine students performing the actual exchange of letters between Abigail Adams and John Adams in 1776 when John was involved in writing the American Declaration of Independence. Imagine students writing and then performing fictional dialogues between characters they have read about in trade books. For example, what kind of conversation might Dr. DeSoto and Sylvester (two William Steig characters from different books—*Dr. DeSoto*, 1990, and *Sylvester and The Magic Pebble*, 1970) have if Sylvester happened to show up one afternoon in Dr. DeSoto's office with a toothache? What sort of dialogues might ensue if President George Washington should happen to show up one day magically in the office of President Barack Obama? Writing such dialogues would require some sophisticated and creative thinking (comprehension), as well as research for the students who would write them. And, of course, the practice and eventual performance of such dialogues would be sure to build fluency as the performers would have to work to make the characters come alive through their voices.

There are also other monologues and dialogues available by looking for favorite parts in movie scripts spoken by one or more characters. Years ago, before my students knew about conducting searches on the Internet, a student named Alan locked himself in his bedroom and put in the DVD of the second movie of the *Lord of the Rings: The Motion Picture Trilogy* (2004). He painstakingly stopped and started the movie, writing down the conversation between Gollum and Sméagol, the two sides of one Tolkien character. Then, he stood in front of his mirror at home and practiced his own interpretation of this wonderful script:

> Gollum: *We wants it, we needs it. Must have the precious. They stole it from us. Sneaky little Hobbitses. Wicked, tricksy, false!*
>
> Sméagol: *No. Not master!*
>
> Gollum: *Yes, precious, false! They will cheat you, hurt you, LIE.*
>
> Sméagol: *Master is our friend!*
>
> Gollum: *You don't have any friends; nobody likes you!*
>
> Sméagol: *I'm not listening...I'm not listening...*
>
> Gollum: *You're a liar and a thief...*

And Alan became known as "Gollum" in our room. He developed this very evil, gutteral Gollum voice contrasted with the sweeter, kinder Sméagol and learned to even change his facial expression for each side of his character.

There are times when we keep our focus on struggling readers during a discussion on reading fluency, but Alan is a wonderful case in point for the benefit to all readers, even the shy ones. Alan was smart, one of the most intelligent children I have ever taught. But he was another one of those painfully shy, bookish kind of students who wanted to stay in the background while reading science books. In fact, during a parent conference at the beginning of fourth grade, I commented to Alan's parents that I could foresee him becoming valedictorian one day. Alan was sitting over in the corner reading a book as we talked. Soon I heard a sniffling in the corner. It was Alan crying. "I don't want to be a valedictorian because they have to give a speech at graduation," he said. At the end of the school year, Alan had become Gollum and performed his perfectly rehearsed dialogue for anyone who would listen! Bright kids benefit from fluency practice, too, especially when we keep our sights on a rich definition of what practice is all about!

Poetry

Because the ultimate goal in any reading activity is deep comprehension, it is important to focus on how to practice one of the most difficult genres to interpret dramatically. Whether the poem is arranged as a reader's theater script, a choral reading, or as a monologue, students seem to struggle with pulling the meaning from the poem and communicating that meaning in the performance.

Poetry Comprehension

One day during reading time, I introduced a poem by Langston Hughes called "Alabama Earth" (1932). From an overhead transparency, I read the poem to the children so they could all see it as I read it aloud. As I finished the read through, one brave girl from my class had the courage to let out a hearty, "HUH?" The rest of the class burst out laughing. I immediately responded to her with, "Why did you say that?" She stumbled around, feeling put on-the-spot I'm sure. I quickly jumped in with "Congratulations! That is what you are supposed to say after reading a poem just once!" I turned to the class and said, "Anna Grace is the most honest person in here. How many of you were silently saying the same thing?" The whole class raised their hands.

How many educated adults, like those reading this text right now, say, "HUH?" after reading most thoughtful poetry through for the first time? It's the right thing to say. That unknowing comment drives us right back to the text because we are motivated to burrow in until we have found the meaning for us buried deep within those words. But children who struggled to make it through the poem the first time will need to be shown our techniques for making the text manageable by chunking the words into phrases as we move toward making meaning of the words. When talking about fluency and the need for rereading to establish fluency in readers, poetry is a natural choice.

Poetry is also a natural for comprehension as poetry deals with metaphor. When Walt Whitman wrote about "My Captain" (1855), he was creating a metaphor for President Lincoln. And when Langston Hughes wrote "Mother to Son" (1922), he wasn't simply describing the difficulty in walking up a flight of stairs, but the challenges that one faces in life's journey. The ability to understand, create, and explore metaphors is a high-level comprehension skill. Using poetry with students is a natural for developing and exploring fluency, vocabulary, and comprehension.

Reading a Poem

Because exposure to poetry begins early, most students equate the reading of poetry with rhyming lines:

I have a little shadow that goes in and out with ME
And what could be the use of me is more than I could SEE!

Rhyming poetry is obviously great for developing phonemic awareness, teaching onset and rimes (word families), and for reading a new word at the end of a line using both context clues and the beginning sound for a word already anticipated through rhyme. And the chant that goes along with reciting or reading aloud a wonderfully written, rhyming poem gives children the idea that with *all* poetry comes a marching rhythm.

They also come into the reading of a poem with the idea that each line holds a complete thought or maybe it is carried in two lines as soon as you attack that last word in the line. After we have worked through curriculum-related poetry in class, I often have each student partner with another student to either rehearse the poem as a choral reading, to practice performing it individually with the other as a coach, or to arrange the poem into meaningful chunks for performance. Early in the process of learning to read poetry in our classroom, as students partner to create their own performances of poetry, they still seem to have a magnetic attraction to sharing a free form poem in one-line sections or couplets of lines even if the meaning only comes with a third line added.

Looking closely at the way students create their own oral performance from an intact piece of poetry is a wonderful window into their ideas about meaning versus simply speaking a rhythm. See pages 69–70 for examples of how the first verse of Robert Frost's poem "The Road Not Taken" (1920) arranged in a variety of ways, illustrates this point.

First poor example of reader's theater using "The Road Not Taken" (Frost 1920):

"The Road Not Taken"
by Robert Frost

Reader 1: Two roads diverged in a yellow wood,

Reader 2: And sorry I could not travel both

Reader 1: And be one traveler, long I stood

Reader 2: And looked down one as far as I could

Reader 1: To where it bent in the undergrowth;

Second poor example of reader's theater:

Reader 1: Two roads diverged in a yellow wood,
And sorry I could not travel both

Reader 2: And be one traveler, long I stood
And looked down one as far as I could

Readers 1
and 2: To where it bent in the undergrowth

Third poor example of a monologue:

Two roads diverged in a yellow wood,

And sorry I could not travel both

And be one traveler, long I stood

And looked down one as far as I could

To where it bent in the undergrowth;

In each of the three arrangements, even after we have studied how to group phrases for meaning, children seem to run back to the rhyme and line to arrange for performance. Interestingly, when I have done this in workshops with teachers, the tendency is to do the same thing. And if I am truly honest, when I first began arranging poetry for my children to perform on Fridays, I thought poetry was the easiest to arrange. I would whip around the class and assign each child a line and I was done with it.

When a poem is arranged and interpreted dramatically for meaning, life and meaning are breathed back into the poem. As I have read about Robert Frost and his love to perform his own poetry, I have learned that he liked to read a poem as if the lines just came to him…as if he was thoughtfully writing it as he spoke the words aloud. Using that insight into Frost's performance style, read his poem in this new arrangement.

A good example of a monologue:

Two roads diverged in a yellow wood (pause)

And sorry I could not travel both and be one traveler,

Long I stood and looked down one as far as I could to where it bent in the undergrowth.

In this new arrangement for one voice, the rhyme and the lines have been minimized for the sake of the meaning. As students see us play with poetry, they begin to realize that the form sometimes hides the meaning. There is a certain thrill to discovering meaning underneath the wraps of a poem.

Poetry Read-Around

In keeping with the goal of reading a poem for meaning before performing it, I learned a wonderful technique from Judy Goodpasture, a high school English teacher in Wichita, Kansas. It's called Poetry Read-Around. I've used it so much that I'm not sure it is exactly the way Judy initially explained it to me, but I love this technique. It works in a large class setting or in a targeted-reading group.

Introduce to the students a poetry reading technique called Read-Around. The purpose of this exercise is to help students see how thoughts in a poem may wrap around lines or may be found in a short phrase. First, the teacher chorally reads the poem with the students to be sure each child is comfortable with word pronunciation. Each student will read a line until a punctuation mark is reached. Immediately, the next student will pick up where the first student stopped and read until the next punctuation mark. Continue until the entire poem is read.

Following this oral reading of the poem, students pull out highlighters and mark the sections between the punctuation marks to visually show the chunks of meaning. The students then pair up with one other person to read it a third time, this time focusing on "shaping the phrase" to show with voice inflections the meaning of the poem.

In one of my workshops at a school in Florida, a school administrator came up to me during a break. She told me that she had chosen "The Road Not Taken" by Robert Frost as her senior poem, having loved it all through high school. But until she participated in the Read-Around exercise and the partner reading during the workshop, she had missed some of the deeper meanings in the verses.

In this age of accountability and year-end assessments, teachers often say, "It's the poetry that is so difficult!" Maybe it is because we are not spending enough time learning to read a poem and digging for the deep meaning in it by looking at its structure and interpreting the phrases.

Improvisational Poetry Reading

Improvisational poetry performance, like the name implies, is done on the fly. Two or more readers are asked to read (perform) a poem together. However, each reader chooses in advance whatever lines, phrases, or words to read on his or her own, without letting the other reader(s) know. Some lines will be read by one reader, some lines by more than one reader. And, of course, there is always the possibility that some lines are not planned to be read by any readers, in which case one or more of the readers need to jump in and read in order to save the reading. Improvisational poetry performances are fun because they are never the same, and they can be a bit of a risk for the performers and the audience.

Songs

Songs may be the lost literature piece in our classrooms today. It seems that unless a teacher was a music teacher in a former life or a weekend performer, the song lyrics are left at home. While an in-house music teacher may meet with your students weekly, they are quickly becoming the victims of budget cuts. And, it is difficult for them to focus on the fluency benefits of song when they have a whole curriculum piece to cover in a very limited time.

When incorporating songs in the regular classroom, it is helpful to think of them married to the word block. Songs are full of rich language, just as poetry is. Songs are also full of rhyme and are fine fodder for word family discussion. Because of the rich language in the song lyrics, a "word harvest" is a wonderful way to gather up vocabulary that the children choose. When doing a word harvest, students simply choose words that are interesting to them. These words are placed on a classroom chart and all week the words are the topic of word play.

Songs can be chosen to fit with seasons or with topics of study. Right now in my fifth grade class, we are learning a set of songs contained in "Vintage Americana" from SingReadLearn (http://www.singreadlearn.com) I have put the songs into chronological order to enhance our study of the history of America. Last week, we sang "Hush Little Baby" (and discussed how the song could have been used to rock George Washington to sleep.) In a few weeks, we will be singing "Boatman Dance" as we discuss the river trade during the early 1800s. Teachers in earlier grades may just choose to sing songs that kids should know or songs that match the season.

Start the week off with a song by introducing it and displaying it for all of the students to see. It is very important that each student track the words of the text, whether on a display or using their own individual texts.

The teacher may give some background information for the song and then the class sings through it, listening to the recording or the teacher's lead. The class sings it together several times, noticing different bits of word knowledge each time. They may notice rhyming patterns, text structure, and interesting words. The students may also discuss the mood of the song as they sing and the author's purpose for putting those words in that setting. Of course, we want our students to comprehend the song early on, so we will want to have a discussion of the meaning behind the song.

All of this learning can take place on one day, or it can be spread out over a whole week. But it is worth noting how all of the parts of our reading curriculum have already been covered in this generic lesson plan for a song. If you choose to teach most of it on Mondays, then the rest of the week can be simply song time for 5–10 minutes a day. If you like the idea of fitting it into a fluency block, then you would divide up the activities into a weekly plan.

Points to Ponder

1. Talk about one of the skills you were required to practice in your early years and relate it to coaching your children to be fluent readers through practice for an authentic purpose of performance.

2. Discuss the flow from dependent, supported reading toward independent, confident reading as told from choral reading to monologues. How do you see this fitting into the grade level or resource area where you teach?

3. Describe some of the roadblocks you have to navigate when teaching poetry comprehension to your students. How do you see the teaching of "reading" a poem as helping with that task?

Chapter 5: Organizing and Preparing for Fluency Instruction

As the car passes the sign "Welcome to North Carolina," I take one last look at summer vacation through the rear view mirror. It happens every year. It is a moment when I realize this respite from work is almost over. July is fleeting. Three weeks stand between the children, the classroom, and me. It's time to get into "school mode."

Each year I step into that school state of mind in a similar way. I think about my successes the year before—the "best-ever moments" that I want to replicate if possible. I think about times when I spotted weak areas in my students' learning and I determine to do things differently. I think about the nitty-gritty things like schedules for my days and a sequence for my weeks. Curriculum is never far away—what new strategies will I learn, in what direction will the pendulum swing in my district, what topics will I teach in each grading period?

But for the last number of years, one of the joys in that last remnant of summer has been to begin to think about fluency instruction. How will I set up my classroom routine in order to teach my students to be fluent readers? How will I organize my year as I attempt to intentionally work on creating confident, fluent, comprehending readers?

This chapter is divided into three major sections. We will be discussing the routine that happens in the days of the week, a master plan for the whole school year, and then zero in on a fluency-filled day.

Back to the Beginning—
A Simple Weekly Routine

In the year 2000 when I first began teaching fluency in my classroom, I had a weekly routine. The routine was simple and effective. I was very new to the idea of using reader's theater scripts, and reader's theater was the only pathway to fluency that I knew about, so my planning was limited. Finding scripts at a challenging but doable reading level for the fourth-grade level was challenging. With my limited collection of scripts in hand, I chose one script for the first week. Without even reading the reader's theater script aloud to the children, I simply handed it out on Monday. My only preparation was to run copies of the script and highlight the parts. In other words, I took the script on the top of the pile and using a yellow highlighter, I marked all "Reader 1" parts. I took the next script and marked all of the "Reader 2" parts. When I arrived at the last part, possibly "Reader 6," I simply changed highlighter colors and started all over again with marking parts. The colors would later assign the students to groups.

The marked parts were handed out to each student in the class, without much concern for individual reading levels. Because all of my students were at least on a low second-grade reading level, I decided that every child in my fourth-grade class could learn to read at least a few lines of just about anything!

As I formed groups each week, I did try to have a truly heterogeneous group on Friday. The performance would drag if all of the children in one group were struggling readers at the beginning of the year. When the groups were of mixed abilities, the lower readers rose to the occasion as they rehearsed with fellow students who modeled the script well. The number of parts on the script determined how many students were in each group. So nothing was permanent and each group's size and membership changed each week.

The kids were given a week-long homework assignment: practice your parts until you know them. Be ready to perform on Friday! On Friday afternoons, the kids gathered into their groups. Remember when I handed out the highlighted parts on Monday? I had used a different color highlighter for each set of scripts. All of the parts highlighted in yellow would now become the members of the "yellow" group. The parts highlighted in pink were now the "pink" group. They rehearsed a few times in groups as I circulated to coach rehearsals. Then they performed. We clapped and ate cookies!

At the very beginning of my first year, the limited number of scripts actually worked to the class's advantage. There was a healthy competitiveness that would rise up as one group heard the other group perform the same lines they were about to present. The group that followed would try to top the previous group. By the end of the session, the first group was just dying to get up there and top them all.

But as that first year moved into the fourth and fifth weeks, I found that the kids were becoming restless with hearing the weekly script over and over again on Friday. So I had to branch out and begin to arrange scripts from stories in the basal or from poems. By the end of the year, I had found enough to keep the kids busy and working hard. There were some scripts that I had arranged like "The Midnight Ride of Paul Revere" (Longfellow 1863) that kept the kids challenged for weeks and since it was arranged for 27 voices, it kept them involved.

Now that I look back on that first year, I am very grateful that my kids showed such tremendous interest and growth. I realize that the key was probably keeping up the routine of weekly performances and not paying a whole lot of attention to the reading levels of my children when I handed out the parts. With all of that practice in reading, they stretched. In fact, one of the students who had been in a targeted Title I group since first grade tested out of Title I within 10 weeks. He had never been stretched to such a degree of expectation and did not know he could do it.

What I learned my first year...

- Fluency must be part of a weekly routine and not a "once in a while" activity.

- Time needs to be spent with the teacher modeling the script before assigning it to the student to take home. The teacher should read the script aloud while the students whisper read or read silently along. There is no reason for the student to sight read the script on his or her own.

- The typical script needs to be relatively short, two or three pages, and have a similar number of lines for each participant. This keeps all of the students challenged and involved in tracking the script.

- Scripts with one student as the "main character" are very effective for teaching content and wide performance. An example of one such script is the "Ain't I a Woman" script, but it should be handled carefully. The initial rehearsal with the main character should take place with a one-on-one coach or parent so that the other students don't spend their rehearsal time listening to another student rehearsing. The longer parts can be at the upper end of the students' reading level because of the nature of multiple rehearsals, but should not be at a high frustration level.

- Most students will learn to read the whole script by tracking even though they are not assigned all of the parts to read.

- Students who are struggling need more support for rehearsing than they may get at home in the evening. Often, their reading struggles stem from having limited language support at home and limited time with an adult reading with them.

The Years That Followed—
An Enhanced Routine

Ever since my first year of teaching fluency, I have been absolutely convinced that fluency instruction doesn't just happen. It must be planned for in advance and must become part of the classroom routine. Reader's theater is not something to be thrown into the curriculum around a holiday. Although it is a "fun activity," it does not accomplish the task of creating fluent readers unless it is an integral part of your reading instruction.

Because of fluency's profound effect on my struggling readers' growth, fluency instruction has become more than a weekly routine in my classroom; it is now a daily one. When I first began, I was afraid to take valuable classroom time to have the students practice parts. I limited it to a take-home assignment and a Friday performance. Now I know that my most needy students may be struggling because there is no one at home with the time and/or the proficiency to effectively coach their reading.

Coaching a struggling reader can be done by a stronger reader in the classroom, a volunteer, a teacher assistant, or the teacher himself or herself. When I coach a student, I first look to see that the student can decode all of the words. But I quickly move into the interpretation of the text. I find that the lack of phrasing for meaning is the greatest pitfall in reading aloud. If a student does not see or hear those implied phrases in a challenging text, he or she will not make meaning and he or she will not be able to read with dramatic expression. Echo reading is effective for demonstrating where the phrases begin and end naturally and how the phrase should be interpreted to give meaning. After a very short coaching session, a student will often grasp the idea of the part and move along quickly to performance level.

I also know that students and parents need more input than simply, "Read this script each night and practice it until you know it well for Friday." The first script of the year has become about the homework routine of practicing reader's theater. At the beginning of the year, the parents are focused on trying to figure out this newly assigned teacher, so this script serves as a means of effective parent communication in addition to teaching the students about my expectations.

"A Reader's Theater for Five Voices"
by Lorraine Griffith

Reader 1: My teacher just told me we were going to do something called "Reader's Theater" this year!

Readers 2–5: We LOVE IT!

Reader 1: What is reader's theater?

Reader 2: It's acting with your voice!

Reader 3: It's telling a story without any props

Reader 4: ...or costumes

Reader 5: ...or scenery!

Reader 1: Do you mean the story is like a movie in your mind?

Readers 2–5: Yes! What a perfect description!

Reader 2: And if the story is frightening, your voice is scary.

Reader 3: If the story is amazing, your voice shows you are flabbergasted.

Reader 1: Flabbergasted?

Readers 2–5: FLABBERGASTED!

Reader 2: We love to use fantastic words!

Reader 4: But if the story is sad, your voice is heartbreaking.

Reader 5: And if the story is happy, you sound thrilled to pieces!

Reader 1: But how do you memorize all those lines in just one week?

Reader 2: You don't! My teacher says, "Never memorize your lines because you will quit working on the meaning of the text!"

Reader 1: How do you practice then if you aren't memorizing the lines?

Reader 3: On Mondays, we practice pro-nun-ci-a-tion!

Reader 4: On Tuesdays, we make sure our parts have a flow, like a rolling river so people can hear the meaning...

Reader 2: ...instead of just a jumble of words.

Reader 5: On Wednesdays, we work on making the words expressive!

Reader 3: Wednesdays make us feel like movie stars, because we love to be dramatic!

Reader 2: On Thursdays, we practice projecting our voices, making them loud enough, so everyone in the audience can hear our lines.

Reader 3: I've even learned to whisper loud enough for everyone to hear me in the back of the room.

Reader 1: How do you practice saying your lines at the right time?

Reader 3: Sometimes I practice with my mom or dad...

Reader 4: ...but sometimes I just practice alone in front of the mirror in my bedroom.

Readers 2–5: And then on Fridays, we perform!

Readers 2, 4: Sometimes we read poetry,

Readers 3, 5: Sometimes we read humorous stories,

Reader 2: Sometimes we read non-fiction, informational selections.

Readers 3–5: But we always have fun!

ALL: Because we LOVE reader's theater!

The enhanced routine has also become more about a variety of fluent reading methods as opposed to simply being relegated to reader's theater practice and performance. Songs and poetry have moved into the instructional routine with equal focus for accomplishing a richer and deeper experience with fluency practice. All students learn in different ways, and the learning of each student is enhanced by presenting instruction in a variety of ways and genres.

I find that songs are wonderful for fluency instruction at the beginning of the year. Students are eased chorally into the art of keeping up with the accurate and automatic decoding of words by reading rhythmically while adding wonderful vocabulary to their language. The genres of song, like the folk song or ballad, are discussed and comprehension study is carried out on the first instructional day of the song. Games are played with words from the songs through word ladders or word construction. The songs are generally enjoyed and help ease the students into reading, utilizing a genuine community-building fluency tool. The song block for fluency fits perfectly with the word block.

Poetry is also studied during a sizable block of the school year as an opportunity to explore the wonderful language and inferring inherent in the way poetry is written. Because meaningful phrases are signaled by the punctuation in poetry and not necessarily the divides of lines, I have found that the keys to finding meaning in poetry must be taught directly to students. After the poem is taught during the teacher-directed reading time, the student can practice and perform the poem with confidence and dramatic flair.

Planning and Organizing for the Whole Year—Creating a Master Plan

State standards, district requirements, and grade-level sequences are the basis of planning a year's curriculum. Once that curriculum is laid out for the school year, a teacher can determine how fluency will be added to, integrated with, and "infused" into subject matter.

In this high-stakes, high-expectations, high-pressure era of education, a teacher friend of mine said, "There is no way I can get this all in. They aren't giving me more time. I'll just have to think smarter." Although I have been teaching with a focus on fluency for 10 years, it looks a little different each year. Fluency instruction has evolved in my classroom to embrace the content curriculum through reader's theater scripts infused with math, science, reading, or social studies. But I now include songs, poetry, and writer's craft passages with dramatic potential in my collection of texts to be used.

Planning the Year by Themes

When the school year is mapped out by topics and themes to be covered, it is helpful to create a set of file folders on your computer or in your file cabinet. Then, as you find songs, poems, passages, and reader's theater scripts, you can collect texts that fit your topics to use throughout the year. All of the songs, poems, and scripts in our *Building Fluency through Practice and Performance* series (Rasinski and Griffith 2007) also have a CD containing the texts in *Microsoft Word*® documents. These documents can simply be saved and dropped into the right computer file folders as a starting point. See Figure 5.1 on the following page for a sample file collection.

Figure 5.1 Sample File Collection for the Civil War

Reader's theater scripts:

- "Events in the History of James W. C. Pennington: Formerly a Slave," from *Building Fluency Through Practice & Performance, American History*
- "Voices from the Civil War," from *Building Fluency Through Practice & Performance, American History*
- "Gettysburg and Mr. Lincoln's Speech," from *Building Fluency Through Practice & Performance, American History*
- "Uncle Tom's Cabin," from *Building Fluency Through Practice & Performance*, Grade 5
- "A Poet's Role in History," from *Building Fluency Through Practice & Performance*, Grade 5
- "Prelude to the Civil War," from *Texts for Fluency Practice*, Grades 4 and up
- "What to the American Slave is Your Fourth of July," from *Texts for Fluency Practice*, Grades 4 and up
- "Drum Taps," from *Texts for Fluency Practice*, Grades 4 and up
- "Sojourner Truth and the Struggle for People's Equality," from *Texts for Fluency Practice*, Grades 4 and up

Songs:

- "The Underground Railcar," from *Building Fluency Through Practice & Performance, American History*
- "Follow the Drinking Gourd," from *Building Fluency Through Practice & Performance*, Grade 4
- "Goober Peas," from *Building Fluency Through Practice & Performance*, Grade 4
- "The Battle Hymn of the Republic," from *Texts for Fluency Practice*, Grades 4 and up
- "I Heard the Bells on Christmas Day," from *Texts for Fluency Practice*, Grades 4 and up

- "The Abolitionist Hymn," from *Building Fluency Through Practice & Performance*, Grade 6
- "The Battle Cry of Freedom," "Battle Hymn of the Republic," "When Johnny Comes Marching Home," from open source Internet searches

Poetry:
- "The Slave's Lament," from *Building Fluency Through Practice & Performance*, Grade 5
- "O Captain, My Captain!" from *Texts for Fluency Practice*, Grades 4 and up
- "Eliza Crossing the River," from *Building Fluency Through Practice & Performance*, Grade 6

Monologues:
- "Company Aytch," from *Building Fluency Through Practice & Performance, American History*
- "Lincoln's Second Inaugural Address," from *Building Fluency Through Practice & Performance*, Grade 4
- "Narrative of the Life of Frederick Douglass, an American Slave," from *Building Fluency Through Practice & Performance*, Grade 5
- "Lincoln's Letter to Mrs. Bixby, 1864," from *Building Fluency Through Practice & Performance*, Grade 5
- "Sullivan Ballou, Letter." available from http://www.PBS.org, http://www.pbs.org/civilwar/war/ballou_letter.html

Speeches: (Available from American Rhetoric, http://www.americanrhetoric.com)
- Abraham Lincoln's *Gettysburg Address*
- Abraham Lincoln's *Cooper Union Speech*
- Abraham Lincoln's *First Inaugural Address*
- Abraham Lincoln's *Second Inaugural Address*
- Jefferson Davis's *Inaugural Address*

Planning the Year by Genre

Different genres for teaching fluency are effective for students in varying stages of reading. Songs, reader's theater scripts, and poetry are all effective means to the end of creating fluent readers. One way of organizing the school year is to divide the school year into thirds, made up of 12-week periods. The year is then planned, focusing on just one genre at a time. For example, you could arrange your year like this:

Weeks 1–12: Songs

Weeks 13–24: Reader's theater

Weeks 25–36: Poetry

The strength of this approach is the streamlining of planning for the year. You are able to choose one genre, such as songs. The songs are then correlated to your study or used in a general way for energizing your students for learning in the mornings or after lunch. The class does not have an opportunity to get tired of one genre because after they master the text type, you move to another, such as the reader's theater script. They will be delighted to have "solo" parts as they try their wings as fluent readers. And then, just as they become settled into the reader's theater scripts, you move them toward choosing their own poetry to share with the class in a solo or duet format. By choosing to move the school year through by genre, you are also giving the students a genuine comfort level in performing in front of a crowd. By beginning with a corporate performance with songs or choral readings, you are not asking students to individually perform. As the year moves on, students are asked to take on more and more of the responsibility for performance.

Songs

Students in the lower grades always lose some of their sight word vocabulary and decoding knowledge over the summer. The students in the upper grades often come in rusty with reading. By focusing on songs at the beginning of the year, students sense that the year is going to be energy filled and they will hardly even notice all of the reading that they are doing with the songs they sing. Songs also lend themselves to "vocabulary harvesting" (and putting words on the classroom word wall for display and use) and "word-building" as you begin the year with assessing where your kids are with decoding words, sight word vocabulary, and defining vocabulary in context. As songs are sung together, a community is being built with common cultural literacy that bonds students and teacher.

Reader's Theater

Once the students have sung together, they will be ready to track the words for the whole script and perform on their own for smaller parts. They bring to the reader's theater script an eye for detecting and harvesting words that they find interesting or difficult to pronounce. By reading through it together at the beginning of the week or performance cycle, the experience is much the same as previewing a song. Students are confident with learning new text.

Poetry

To interpret a poem with true interpretive voice and phrasing, a student has to develop some confidence with reading a poem. By having 24 weeks of modeling the reading of poetry before the student is asked to interpret text independently, he or she will be able to come in at a much higher level of practice. Tim always says in his workshop that children begin with the funny poems and move on to deeper, more serious poetry. Eventually, students can and should write their own poems, often emulating the poets that they have performed and loved earlier in the year. And, I have found this to be more true when I focus on poetry during the last part of the school year when they have discovered the joy of finding deep meaning throughout the curriculum all year.

Planning Fluency-Filled Days

Now that you have thought through your year, you may have decided to infuse your day with lots of fluency practice, perhaps with a song in the morning or a poem to close in the afternoon. It could be a fluency development lesson several times each week to make sure you are teaching prosody and expression as the focal points of fluency. It could also be a full-blown poetry unit once or twice during the year. Figure 5.2 below shows a sample weekly lesson plan that infuses fluency throughout the schedule.

Figure 5.2 Weekly Lesson Plan

Monday	Tuesday	Wednesday	Thursday	Friday
8:00 A.M. **Daily:** (10 min.) Song!				
10:00 A.M. (20 min.) Fluency Development Lesson	**10:00 A.M.** (20 min.) Fluency Development Lesson	**10:00 A.M.** (20 min.) Fluency Development Lesson	**10:00 A.M.** (20 min.) Fluency Development Lesson	
2:00 P.M. (10–15 min.) Practice	**2:00 P.M.** (10–15 min.) Practice	**2:00 P.M.** (10–15 min.) Practice	**2:00 P.M.** (10–15 min.) Practice	**2:00 P.M.** (30–40 min.) Grand Performance

8:00 A.M. Song:

Introduce a new song on Monday and have the students sing along with the lyrics that are displayed on an overhead projector. Use the same song all week to introduce new vocabulary to English language learners and struggling readers, to reinforce the sight words as they fly by to a melody, to simply enjoy the community of singers in a classroom, and to set the stage for a positive school day. The song time is a welcome addition to calendar time for primary students or a refreshing introduction to the word block for second through sixth grade.

10:00 A.M. The Fluency Development Lesson (FDL):

The Fluency Development Lesson (FDL) (Rasinski, Padak, Linek, and Sturtevant 1995) is particularly useful with students for whom fluency is a major concern. The FDL employs a daily passage that is rich with opportunity for expression and prosody exploration. The passage can be simply pulled from the reading story you are using during that day or week. It could be a passage from the read-aloud you are using that day. The passage could be a wonderfully written piece from a news article relevant to the topic that you are teaching in one of the content areas. When the passage is connected to writer's craft, it becomes an internalized example of something you want replicated in the students' writing. This lesson format can even be used in kindergarten with the "Morning Message."

At the beginning of the school year, I use the FDL to instruct all of my students at any level of reading ability. By using it with all of your students at the beginning of the year, you are actually multiplying yourself by including the strong readers in the mix of students reading dramatically to one another. The stronger students will model for the weaker students. As the school year moves into the fourth or fifth week, I begin to use it less during my full class instructional time and continue it a few times a week with my struggling readers. Eventually, I use it only with my struggling readers during their small-group time in the afternoon.

As I write this chapter, my fifth graders are beginning a study of the regions of the United States. We are reading poems from the Scholastic book *My America: A Poetry Atlas of the United States* (Hopkins 2000). When my students were reading a poem about the nation's capital ("Washington, D.C.") the assignment for fluency homework was to read the poem to five different people, the "Lucky Listeners," and have each of them sign the back of the poem. By adding a "Lucky Listener" piece to the process, the FDL also goes home in the same day.

The listeners at home can learn numerous important things by listening:

- There is value in rereading a text.

- The students are studying the United States this year and Washington, D.C., in particular. The content has come home for discussion and further exploration.

- Reading aloud is fun!

- The student can read grade-level text!

Synergistic Instruction

Figure 5.3 on page 91 shows a step-by-step process for planning a Fluency Development Lesson (FDL). The FDL (Rasinski et al. 1995) employs relatively short reading passages (poems, rhymes, songs, story segments, or other texts) that students read and reread over a short period of time. The format for the lesson follows a routine of the teacher taking responsibility for reading the daily passage and gradually shifting responsibility for the reading to the students.

Figure 5.3 The Fluency Development Lesson (FDL)

1. The teacher introduces a new short text and reads it to the students two or three times while the students follow along silently. The text can be a poem, segment from a basal passage, or trade book selection, etc.

2. The teacher and students discuss the nature and content of the passage, as well as the quality of the teacher's reading of the passage.

3. Teacher and students read the passage chorally several times. Antiphonal reading and other variations are used to create variety and maintain engagement.

4. The teacher organizes students into pairs or trios. Each student practices the passage three times while his or her partner listens and provides support and encouragement.

5. Individuals and groups of students perform their reading for the class or other audience such as another class, a parent visitor, the school principal, or another teacher.

6. The students and their teacher then choose four to five interesting words from the text to add to the individual students' word banks and/or the classroom word wall.

7. Students engage in 5–10 minutes of word study activities (e.g., word sorts with word bank words, word walls, flash card practice, defining words, word games, and so on).

8. The students take a copy of the passage home to practice with parents and other family members.

9. The following day, students read the passage from the previous day to the teacher or a fellow student for accuracy and fluency. Words from the previous day are also read, reread, grouped, and sorted by students and groups of students. Students may also read the passage to the teacher or a partner who checks for fluency and accuracy.

The instructional routine then begins again with Step #1 using a new passage.

2:00 P.M. Weekly Practice or Grand Performance:

Try to choose reader's theater scripts that correlate with the topics you will be teaching during that grading period. This allows you to fit reader's theater into a fully scheduled day without making it an additional learning block. For example, if I am teaching the American Revolution in my social studies block, I can use the "Tories, Revolutionaries, and Neutrals" script from Texts for Fluency Practice (Rasinski and Griffih 2009) during Directed Reading, during social studies, or even during Guided Reading to focus on reading text with expression and phrasing. During my mathematics unit on data, I may use the "Working with Data" script for a week or two at the beginning of the math block. Figure 5.4 on the following page shows how to incorporate reader's theater into the weekly schedule.

Figure 5.4 A Daily Routine for Reader's Theater in the Classroom

Monday

Display the script for the class to see. This can be done with a document camera, an interactive whiteboard, or an overhead projector. Read the script aloud with the class for them to follow and grasp the whole of the text. The goal at the beginning is for the students to comprehend the text. Take the time for the readers to chorally read or echo read the whole text as you read through it the second time. Some teachers play audio recordings of the reader's theater for students to have as a fluent model for the expression of the voices in the script.

Tuesday–Thursday

Next, it is time for the students to learn their parts. If the whole class is performing the same script, then there will probably be four or five performances on Friday. Rehearse homogeneously for the first few rehearsals, where students with the same part are grouped together. When the students seem to be grasping the parts and showing strong interpretation of the text, put the students into heterogeneous groups where there is only one person for each part. The students practice for about 10 minutes each day.

Friday

On this day, plan for a longer block of time, perhaps in place of the FDL. This is a time when each reader is given the chance to be the star. Students perform for each other, sometimes for other classes, and often for parents. All of the students can learn from each other, so they are instructed to look for star qualities or positive behaviors to comment about after each group completes its performance. Students should be honest with each other, learning to recognize improvements as they work on various qualities such as expression, pacing, and word pronunciation throughout the year.

Performance days are when the teacher's and students' imaginations can soar! There are no limits to the way these times can be designed. In another chapter, we will share some of the creative ideas for performance.

Conclusion

As a new school year begins, it is very important to have a plan. In the first year, you may want to keep it very simple. You may want to choose songs or poems as your fluency instruction text for the whole year, instead of the way I began with reader's theater. The most important thing is to have a routine that is weekly and is easily woven into your day. As your style of teaching fluency and your preferences of texts evolve, your classroom technique and performances may look very different than mine. But, if the focus of instruction is on reading text with dramatic expression, model phrasing, and a growing love for the deeper meaning of the written word, you have done your job as a reading fluency teacher.

Points to Ponder

1. Do you have any memories of reading poetry, scripts, songs, and other alternative forms of texts in your own school experience? Did you think of these as reading experiences? Did you find them enjoyable?

2. If you could devote 15–20 minutes per day to fluency instruction, how would you reorganize your day? Your week? Your year?

3. What kinds of texts appeal to you for developing both the automaticity and prosodic elements of fluency?

Chapter 6: Coaching—The Missing Piece

The ideas about teaching with a reading fluency focus found within this book have been shared with hundreds of teachers in workshop settings. I've used words like *magic* when I describe the dramatic results I have achieved by implementing a focus on interpretive oral reading performance. More than a few times, though, I have had teachers come back to me later and say, "Well, I tried reader's theater with my students and it just didn't work for them! I didn't see the impressive results you had in your classroom." Comments such as these have caused me to go back and examine what was possibly left out of my workshops.

It is my conclusion that the one area of my practice minimized and unarticulated in my sharing with teachers was the coaching element. When I described my process that first year, I would simply say, "I handed out scripts on Monday. They practiced all week at home. We spent time practicing in groups on Friday and then we performed."

What I left out of my discussion was the intensity of the "practicing in groups" part on the days that preceded the Friday performances. It was intense *group coaching* time. The students would perform at the end of the week, but it wouldn't end there. We always ended the performance session with a short discussion time and the performance wrap-ups were intense *coaching-by-modeling* times. Often, I would say things like, "Let's do this again next week, but listen carefully as I read this part again." Or, "*This* is what I mean by getting into your character." Then I would read it again, with drama in my voice demonstrating how I expected them to take it up a notch the next week in practice and performance.

How does this coaching piece look in the classroom setting when fluency is your focus and you want the time spent to yield results? In this chapter, we will be looking specifically at coaching students in a reader's theater performance for the sake of continuity. Note also that these techniques will work with helping students to interpret any oral reading performance, such as poetry and monologues, dialogues, jokes, and more. You would follow the whole routine except for the parts of this chapter that deal with group interaction of parts.

Coaching by Modeling

As we have described in previous chapters, the greatest model for fluent reading in your classroom is you. While doing read-alouds thoughtfully, you are showing how a book is transformed into a real living body of characters and the role your voice plays in exciting plot development. When my students see me caught up in the excitement of a book being read aloud, they lose themselves in the setting with me. I can always tell the reading is going well if we all jump when someone knocks on the door or the phone rings.

When a new script is introduced to a classroom, it is imperative that the teacher give background for the genre, history, and setting of the piece to be read. A reader's theater script written around a historical speech or rooted in cultural events is read very differently than a script featuring a Robert Frost poem. The students need to see the difference in mood set by the author's purpose in writing the piece.

Because our ultimate goal in reading is rich comprehension, a struggling or unmotivated reader will not read interpretively before understanding the main idea of the script and hearing each individual role modeled from the script. As a teacher reads the whole script dramatically for the class, students will see the interplay of the voices and the importance of reading the lines in character.

There are also recordings available of a poet reading his or her own poem or an orator reading his or her own speech. Once we were working with the Abbot and Costello script, "Who's on First?" For some reason we could not master the appropriate timing and humor. We bumbled our way through it for a whole week. Finally, our teacher assistant brought in a recording of the comedy routine. We tried to follow a labeled baseball field diagram on the board as fast as Abbott and Costello ran through the lines and suddenly, the students understood the humor. From that moment, the kids were infected with the desire to read it as well as hear the recording. We ended up competing with another class for the best interpretation of the script, and one of our English language learners (also a struggling reader) was in the winning pair of readers!

Coaching in Homogeneous Groups

When you are using the same script with all of the readers in your class, you will have multiple students on the same part. We have previously suggested that the students spend some time rehearsing with their peers on the same assigned part. In other words, all of the narrators will meet together in one group as each of the other parts meet in their own respective groups.

Usually, this rehearsal time is spent in choral reading the parts. Choral reading or echo reading is very helpful with pronunciation of words. As soon as the readers have mastered the pronunciations of each word in the parts, I would move to phrasing. Students do not necessarily pause even when a comma or period dictates the pause. But harder still is when there is a long line of dialogue with no punctuation indicating thoughtful breaks.

As you work with this small group, you will want to also think with them about their role in the script. A narrator part is a storyteller and has plenty of potential for dramatic expression. If they have a character part, though, they will need to be sure to understand the character's role in this part of history or in the story. From all of this discussion with each individual part will eventually come the overall mood of the piece.

Coaching Individually

Coaching individually does not necessarily require pulling each student one by one to work with each alone. In fact, the other day, our whole grade level was working on a production of reader's theater for parents. In all, there were 44 parts. At the end of the whole grade level rehearsal, I had the 44 individual readers crowd into my classroom, and we drilled parts. Very few of the students were interpreting their parts with power, and few of them knew how to focus on important words or enjoy the spectacular dramatic pause. And for the next hour, I worked with them individually! I put a bucket of lollipops at the front of the room and said, "Do I have any volunteers to go first?" It was almost lunchtime and the lollipops were alluring, so I had a few students who bravely raised their hands to try parts.

Here's the tricky part. John Wooden, the great basketball coach, is often credited with saying, "A coach is someone who can give correction without causing resentment." As I work with students in front of other students, I try my best to correct without defeating. A good teacher can see the difference between challenging and breaking a student.

So what happens if a child stands and reads the part poorly? I would say, "Wow! I think you know how to pronounce every word, but those words are *powerful* and I need to hear that power. Try it again and this time I want you to punch these three words!" The script is displayed for all of the class to see the marking of a script. Using a document camera to display the script in my room, I place slashes where I want pauses and circles around the words I want the student to emphasize. Then, we rehearse it again.

What happens next is beautiful. Because the next student sees how the previous student's part took on new life, he or she is already a step ahead. He or she reads with power, needs a little help with phrasing and emphasized words, grabs his or her lollipop, and we're off to the next student.

I want to slip in a word about the dramatic pause. Recall the opening to *A Tale of Two Cities* by Charles Dickens (1997) shown below. Read it aloud and think about the power of the comma in your comprehension of the piece.

A Tale of Two Cities
by Charles Dickens

It was the best of times, it was the worst of times, it was the age of wisdom, it was the age of foolishness, it was the epoch of belief, it was the epoch of incredulity, it was the season of Light, it was the season of Darkness, it was the spring of hope, it was the winter of despair, we had everything before us, we had nothing before us....

What a beautiful piece of literature! But, it is a huge mistake to read it without a "pregnant pause" between each phrase. We have to teach our children not to be afraid of silent spaces in their reading. It gives the audience a chance to reflect on the rich meaning of what they are saying.

Now, as a personal exercise, read the passage again with the following boldfaced words emphasized. Hold onto the dramatic pauses and add power to the key words.

*It was the **best** of times, it was the **worst** of times, it was the age of **wisdom**, it was the age of **foolishness**, it was the **epoch** of belief, it was the epoch of **incredulity**, it was the season of **Light**, it was the season of **Darkness**, it was the spring of **hope**, it was the winter of **despair**, we had **everything** before us, we had **nothing** before us....*

Different students have different issues and that is why they have to be coached individually at some point. Some students struggle with articulation, putting beginnings and endings on their words. Other students' voices seem to die off at the end of each sentence. The first part is loud and clear and then it goes down into a pit with the period. Some students rush through parts, and others punch every word without much thought to interpretation. Coaching would be easy if each student were the same. But, students are individuals and may need coaching alone.

From this type of coaching session, the students should have plenty of guidance to practice their parts at home or with a peer at school. The expectation of interpretation for performance has been set and the student is not still simply saying words over and over again. The result of meaningless repetition with no guidance ends with a student trying to say it faster to prove he or she knows it. And, we all know by now, there is very little benefit in racing through text.

Coaching in Heterogeneous Groups

After the students have practiced individually, it is time to put the parts together into a heterogeneous group. There may need to be a recap of the introductory discussion of the cultural background, the historic setting, and the author's purpose in writing the piece. Is the piece supposed to be humorous or serious? Should it be persuading the audience to feel a certain way or to see a different viewpoint from history? Is it simply a beautiful telling of a familiar story? What do we want to communicate in our presentation?

I remember some boys in my class a few years ago who were doing a piece entitled "The Passenger Pigeon" from Paul Fleischman's *I Am Phoenix: Poems for Two Voices* (1989). There was no life to the piece even though they had the pronunciations down and their two voices timed to perfection. Until they realized that it was a piece written about looming extinction, there was no passion. Once they learned the background to the piece and did a few minutes of research, the interpretation kicked in and it turned into a wonderfully inspired performance.

Not everyone gets to be the main voice in a reader's theater production, but everyone has a role in making the piece a rich rendition of the script. As the students begin to rehearse, remind them of the mood that they want to convey. They will need to work on timing their lines, remembering their interpretive phrasing, and having strong voices, so that the audience can hear them speak.

Part of the beauty of this rehearsal is the way the students track the other parts in order to know where they need to come in. I remember a performance of a Robert Longfellow poem that was well above a fourth-grade reading level, but performed beautifully by my fourth graders. We presented it in front of a group of seasoned reading educators. The comment after the presentation was the teachers' corporate thrill at seeing so many of the struggling readers silently mouthing the parts of the entire script in an effort to come in on time. I don't suggest teaching your students to mouth all of the words of the other parts, but it was a visible reminder for me to notice how our struggling readers and English language learners continue to benefit from reader's theater even after they have moved on from just focusing on their own lines.

Coaching Just Before Performing

Just before the performance, students should be encouraged to articulate, speak loudly enough for the audience to hear, emphasize the key words for meaning, and enjoy the production! The scripts should be read, but not held in front of the face so that the voice is muffled. Ideally, the students could have music stands on which to place the scripts, but black folders also work for them to learn to hold as they read above the folder. They should be encouraged to use their facial expression to promote the mood of their voice as they speak. Body and hand gestures can be powerful extensions of communicating without becoming a distraction, all the while keeping the feet in a comfortable position on the floor.

When nerves kick in, my parting reminder is to "slow it down!" Once they are fluent and confident in the part, it is too easy to get caught up in the excitement and then perform the words in the script too fast.

Ending the performance is always a bit uncomfortable when the students don't know what to do. In my classroom, we always clap for the performers and then make a positive comment about what we saw them do. In a more formal performance, you may want to teach them to bow at the completion of the script.

Coaching the Audience

An audience of students will need to be coached on how to be good listeners. If you are doing a classroom performance, you may want the students to jot down a few comments as they listen. The comments can be categorized as positive comments and "I wish" comments. For example, "Juan, your expression was amazing!" "Anna, your part was so sad, and I really felt it!" "I wish I could have heard Amy better." "I wish Tony would have slowed down because I missed part of his speech."

Parents may need to better understand what reader's theater is all about when you have your first performance. They may need to realize that the script is simply interpreted with voice and is not a production with props and costume. You may need to encourage them to listen attentively and to use their imaginations to fill in the period costuming or the set behind the students. Most of all, we want to seize every opportunity to teach parents to be positive listeners for their children's reading. As teachers, we often take for granted that parents know what good reading sounds like. This knowledge is not always there for parents and we need to show them by these practiced examples in performance. This is especially important for the parent of a struggling reader who may for the first time hear his or her child read well. They leave the performance with a new standard for their child's reading, set by the child himself.

Coaching After the Fact

If you are able to record the performance, you will be able to do a football-style playback discussion of what happened during the performance. This could be valuable for your class for the next script, a repeat of the script for the next week, or a model for the students the following year. Knowing your students' capability of taking correction in a positive light is essential here. If you are viewing a performance where a student really fell apart, you may need to completely skip over that performance on the video to prevent further embarrassment. But, if the student is resilient, it can be handled very well and it may be a real turning point in the student's focus on rehearsal and preparation for performance.

Coaching "Carry Over"

This may be the greatest omission on my part when I described the amazing results in my classroom over those first three years. As I focused on Friday performance times during that first year, the coaching element began pervading my teaching of reading all day long. I became a "career coach" and found myself pulling out opportunities to dramatically interpret pieces all day long. I was coaching by example as I read aloud, saying things like, "Wow, I loved that part! I want to read that again and really feel what Ida B must have been feeling there!"

And students become their own peer coaches. Students would coach themselves as they read aloud together in teacher directed reading. They would say, "Let's read that again but use the voices of the characters." And, even as the students read their own narrative writing, we would encourage interpretive reading. My role as a fluent reading coach invaded the classroom and became an integral part of the instructional day.

Closing Thoughts on Coaching

As I look back on my favorite hour of teaching so far this school year, it has to be the hour I spent with the 44 students from several other classes crammed into my room on borrowed chairs. I loved the way they began, saying things to each other like, "Hey, this is really fun!" "I think I get it now!" or to me, "Hey, I want to try this!"

But by far the best hour of any school year would have to be the evening performance with parents. I saw the pride in each student's eyes as they pronounced ridiculously difficult words and phrases like *defamation* or *European domination* with ease and power, communicating the meaning behind the great words of famous people in history. And it all goes back to that hour spent—it was that hour of coaching that made the difference between a meaningless recitation of mediocre word pronunciations and the powerful communication of great ideas. It was the coaching that paved the way for the students to make the great gains in reading through the power of a rich, fluent reading experience.

Points to Ponder

1. Think back to a coach you had in your school days. What were the admirable qualities of a coach that you would want to emulate as you coach your students corporately and individually in reading?

2. Take a few minutes to look at this short performance passage from the first chapter of *Alice's Adventures in Wonderland* by Lewis Carroll (2009). Where would you guide a student to pause and which words would you want him or her to emphasize for optimum comprehension?

Alice's Adventures in Wonderland

by Lewis Carroll

Alice was beginning to get very tired of sitting by her sister on the bank, and of having nothing to do: once or twice she had peeped into the book her sister was reading, but it had no pictures or conversations in it, "and what is the use of a book," thought Alice, "without pictures or conversations?"

So she was considering in her own mind (as well as she could, for the hot day made her feel very sleepy and stupid), whether the pleasure of making a daisy-chain would be worth the trouble of getting up and picking the daisies, when suddenly a white rabbit with pink eyes ran close by her.

3. There were multiple opportunities presented in this chapter to use coaching in the oral reading practice. Where are there other opportunities in your daily routine to coach your students in oral reading?

Chapter 7: Creating Grand Performances

We have talked about multiple ways to practice fluency in the classroom, from chorally reading a speech or poem, to singing, to saying a monologue and practicing a script individually. In all of these ways, students are learning to use phrasing and expression for reading. They are also giving indisputable evidence that they are comprehending text. But in order to continue to motivate students to reach higher—toward a more difficult text and a more dramatic interpretation—they need to *perform* in front of peers and parents.

There is an anecdote about Vladimir Horowitz, the famous piano virtuoso, being asked if he practiced the piano every day. He replied, "Practice? Never! I only rehearse!" If this story is true, Horowitz was always preparing for the next performance. He had a good reason to work at his craft—audiences filled auditoriums to hear him perform.

Horowitz is also purported to have said, "I must tell you I take terrible risks. Because my playing is very clear, when I make a mistake you hear it. If you want me to play only the notes without any specific dynamics, I will never make one mistake. Never be afraid to dare."

Performing is risky. When we are asking our students to put their work out in front of an audience, it is scary for them at first! Articulating the words well and interpreting the text with expression, dynamics, and prosody is personal and risky. As teachers, we have to be willing to put in the rehearsal time so that they come to a performance with confidence.

Performing for an audience adds rich value to the whole experience by giving a real purpose. There are struggling readers and English language learners who have never rehearsed a reading piece well enough to "sound like a fluent reader." But now they have accomplished a new level of reading and need the positive feedback of an audience, as well as the sense of fulfillment that comes from a noteworthy and meaningful performance.

Classroom Performances

Classroom performances are a natural way to provide an audience. Individual and small groups of students, usually in groups of five or six, perform at the front of the room, and the rest of the class listens for evidence of fluent reading. After the first group performs a reader's theater arrangement of Mary Howitt's poem "The Spider and the Fly" (2002), students learn to address a fellow student with respect and to say something like, "Juan, I really like how you sounded so scary when you were the spider. Your voice changed—I had to look twice to see it was really you!" Or, a student could say, "I like how all of you were into the drama of the spider poem and I really didn't even notice that it rhymed." By training students to comment specifically in response to a performance, you are actually reteaching the features of fluent reading. The individual and small groups of performers then each take a turn performing and enjoying the positive feedback from the peers in the audience.

At the beginning of the year, it may be good to have the whole class performing the same script. During the performance, the students will observe one another closely and the performances will become progressively more dramatic as one group follows another. As the year progresses and as your thematic script collection grows, you may want to have multiple scripts performed on Performance Day. For example, if you were doing a unit on literature genres, it would be fun to have scripts that come from the various traditional genres you are teaching. Different small groups could perform different pieces, such as a folktale, a tall tale, a legend, and a fairy tale. When the students have finished for the week, you can always trade the scripts and perform them again the next week with different readers.

Traveling Teams

Traveling Teams can be assigned following the performances in the classroom. "Group Three, you did such a beautiful job on 'Little Orphan Annie!' I'd like for your group to be our Traveling Team next week and go perform for the other third grade classes." This honor of performing the script multiple times is a reward for hard work and is a real motivator for the groups working the following week. Teachers love to have fine examples of fluency modeled by guest stars in their classrooms. Simply display a sign-up sheet with times that suit your classroom's schedule, and other teachers will sign up for a visit from the "stars."

By making arrangements for your Traveling Team to stop in the office, the cafeteria, or the custodians' lounge, you are creating or extending an appreciation for reading fluency throughout the school. The fervor for fluency—real fluency—spreads.

Parental Involvement

Involved parents have been shown to be one of the most important pieces in the success of our students' educational development. There are authentic ways to involve parents in the growth of their children as fluent readers. Of course, the most important thing a teacher can do is to inform and train parents on the importance of reading aloud to their children and encouraging them to dramatically read at home. By doing parent education, the coaching opportunity extends and they can appreciate what they hear in a performance. The parents will begin to view their child as a confident, interpretive reader and build the child's chances for long-term success. Here are some ways to share the children's fluency work at school with the parents at home or in school.

Podcasts

An exciting and fun way to increase parental involvement in the curriculum is through the use of podcasts. The Internet broadcasts student progress to parents, grandparents, and friends across the world. With the technology available in most schools today, this is simply a process of making a recording and uploading the recorded performance to a classroom website. Many students will jump at the chance to learn the technology and can then be made available to help teachers with the recording of pieces and the uploading of the podcast.

Students can listen to each other through the computer or iPod® and feel a real sense of accomplishment by having their own performances published as podcasts. Students' motivation to do well and to read fluently increases with this type of performance. On the other hand, parents can also hear if their child is struggling with reading compared to other students at the same grade level who are at a higher level of reading fluency. When parents are not in the classroom daily and consistently hearing students read at the specific grade level, they simply don't know what a grade-level reader sounds like. By hearing what a solid dramatic performance by an accomplished reader sounds like on the podcast, the student who is struggling can then be coached toward that higher level during rehearsals at home the following week.

Lucky Listeners

Another opportunity for parents to hear their child's developing reading fluency is to use a Lucky Listeners routine. This performance method can be used daily. The students work on reading a poem or dramatically reading a passage during the day at school. The student takes the poem or passage home in the homework folder and reads it to three people that night. The Lucky Listeners sign the back with a comment or two about the reading; the next day, the students turn it in as part of their reading homework. I've seen students come back with a note that they called grandparents in another state to be their Lucky Listeners.

I've even seen a paw print from a pet dog as one of the Lucky Listeners. This is positive parent communication, allowing the parents to see the content of what was taught that day at school and allowing the parents to participate and applaud the child's work in reading.

Special Classroom Visitors

Visitors can be asked to come to your classroom to act as audiences for your students' performances. Students are happy to perform for even an audience of one, as long as that audience is enthusiastic and encouraging. Special visitors might include parents, the school principal, school secretary or nurse, other teachers, even students from other classrooms. Special classroom visitors work particularly well with the fluency development lesson where, after lots of practice, every student in your classroom needs an audience. A positive comment, a hug, or a sticker after the performance is often enough to keep students wanting to keep practicing and performing on subsequent days.

Formal Performances for Parents

Another great opportunity for parental involvement is to have formal performances for parents a few times each year. Although parents are always invited to weekly performances, more parents may choose to make the time to come if the teacher combines the display of classroom projects with a formal poetry performance or reader's theater performance. Displays might include poems and scripts that students have written and will perform that evening. Some schools do these performances in the evening combined with a parent/teacher meeting or a parent education night.

One of my favorite performances happened on the Friday before President's Day. The class decorated the school auditorium with national colors and invited the parents. Each student had been assigned two presidents to research. From the research information, the students were asked to do two creative projects. They first wrote and word processed biographical poetry for each president. Secondly, the students created a museum of artifacts to show a significant contribution by a specific president. For example, the student who had George Washington brought in a candle shaped like the number "1" because he was our first president and had to blaze the way as our first leader in national government. Thomas Jefferson was represented by a homemade quill and inkwell for his contribution to the Declaration of Independence. And a white flag with a giant slash across it was in the museum display for "Unconditional Surrender Grant."

Several of my computer-savvy students created a multimedia presentation showing the official portraits of each president. We used the reader's theater script "From the Mouths and Pens of the American Presidents," from the *American History* version of *Building Fluency Through Practice & Performance* (Rasinski and Griffith 2007). As the reader's theater performance began, each student took a turn walking up to the microphone to read the assigned president's most famous quote. The multimedia ran through the slides as each student read dramatically. It was a tremendously moving performance and the students learned so much about the flow of history and the contributions of presidents as they prepared and performed. This type of performance can be designed around any content-related theme. If your grade level studies state or provincial history, you could choose 25 famous people from your state or province and do the very same kind of presentation. If you teach in the lower grades, you could choose community helpers and create simple but dramatic lines for each child to read. The kindergarten or first grade students could do this kind of presentation with nursery rhymes or the alphabet. The *Building Fluency* series mentioned above also includes selections such as "African Animals," "Nations of the World," "Notable Women from History," "Peacemakers," and "Scientists Who Changed the World."

Creative performances are a wonderful way to show off the content your students have learned and to find an avenue for displaying and celebrating the results of their research studies. Parents love this! Grandparents do, too—maybe even more.

Performance Celebrations

There are many ways to celebrate students' performances. Back in the classroom, adding food to the weekly performance gives a sense of celebration to the reader's theater presentation. You can call the weekly performance "Dinner Theater," or more realistically "Snack Theater," and have refreshments for kids to munch on while they listen to other groups. By having a snack list out at the "Meet the Teacher" celebration at the beginning of school, parents can either sign up to send in a fresh snack on a specified day or send in a packaged snack to use sometime throughout the year.

Inviting classroom buddies from the lower grades to your classroom for performances will also add to the fun and celebratory spirit. Another way to celebrate performance differently is to switch gears completely with a poetry celebration.

Poetry Coffeehouses and Slams

Have you ever gone to a coffeehouse, usually near a college campus, where students, professors, and other would-be poets perform poetry readings—poems that they write, as well as poems written by others? It's a powerful experience. Part of what makes it powerful is the environment or ambiance that goes with the coffeehouse—the coffee, the food, the stool on the stage from which the poets perform, the lowered lighting, the master of ceremonies, the audience response—clapping of hands, snapping of fingers, shouts of encouragement, etc.

Have you ever thought about having a regular coffeehouse in your classroom—say every Friday afternoon, an hour before the end of the school day? I know several teachers who are doing this on a regular basis with their students. Here's how it works:

The poetry coffeehouse begins on Mondays when students select a poem that they would like to perform, either on their own, or with a partner or two. Students select from a variety of sources—online, written anthologies, and the like. Once chosen, the students rehearse their poems all week, trying to read them in such a way that is most engaging and entertaining for the audience.

The payoff comes on Friday when students, often dressed in black, show up wearing berets and bearing bongos and toting tambourines, ready to perform their poems. The excitement builds as the teacher works with students to transform the room into a 1950s or 1960s San Francisco-style coffeehouse. Beads are hung, candles are lit, lights are dimmed, the bar stool is placed center stage. Parents are invited to the performance day and can even be encouraged to read poems themselves. A parent volunteer brings juice and snacks for students and guests to share during the coffeehouse.

And then, for the next 30–40 minutes, students introduce their poems to the audience and then perform, one after another. Audiences respond to all performances with courteous applause and finger snapping. Some performances, often from those students you would least expect it from, are showstoppers.

For students and teachers, this is a special way to end the week, a regular school event that students will remember for the rest of their lives.

Equally important, students are learning to love poetry. Early in the year, they perform the silly and funny poems, but midyear they are urged by their teacher to move toward more serious poems and poets. By the end of the year, students are performing their own poetry, often written in a style of a poet they have read earlier and admire.

And on top of all this, students are developing fluency as they practice their chosen poems—the practice is aimed at expressive and meaningful reading, not speed.

A variation of this is a *poetry slam*. A poetry slam is a competitive poetry performance, which has become very popular in recent years. After each poem is performed, each audience member rates the poet on various aspects of the performance—expression, volume, poise, and overall impact. The Master of Ceremonies tallies the ballots for each performer and at the end of the day, the top three performers, are recognized. The poetry slam challenges students to read with expression and enthusiasm. Some teachers have really liked the idea of poetry slams in their classrooms; others, who prefer not to promote competition, go with the more traditional coffeehouse. Regardless of the format you might use, the idea of performing poetry for a real audience makes this an excellent vehicle for fluency and more.

Whole-School Fluency Celebrations

Reader's Theater

We are beginning to see entire schools embrace the idea of focusing on fluency, and this focus is seen in whole-school fluency celebrations. A school might choose a season of the year, a subject such as science, or a period of history to focus on for performance.

The school where I teach has been doing this for several years. Our entire school performs reader's theater for the parents during the last week of school in December. The theme is winter, and each student is involved in performing for a very large audience. The auditorium is decorated and the microphones are set up for the two weeks of performances. Different grade levels perform on different days. Music is played as parents are seated. Each teacher has each of his or her performance groups cycle through at the microphones as the parents enjoy seeing the students celebrate the winter season. There are refreshments served at the end for the students and their families.

Sing-along

Another way to focus on song lyrics is to choose a set of songs to learn as a school. Throughout a period of time, all of the students learn the song lyrics and maybe even the history behind the songs. Your students and staff will love the end result of singing together as a whole student chorus.

This past year, our whole school focused on song lyrics for 10 weeks of the school year. We learned all the verses of songs such as "Meet Me in St. Louis" (Sterling and Mills 1904), "Hush, Little Baby" (Rasinski and Griffith 2007), and others that reflected the American culture from previous generations.

Then we had a local band come to the school to lead a giant sing-along celebrating the songs we had learned. There were over 800 students and teachers crowded into our gymnasium as we sang as one. It was a tremendous celebration of learning and a newly shared school culture. When the school year ended, our principal said it was one of the best experiences she ever had as an elementary school principal, watching the little kindergartners, the diverse group of special needs students, and the sophisticated fifth graders all singing together with gusto!

It is the performance, whether grand or simple, that makes the practice worthwhile. And it is the practice—real practice aimed at delivering meaning to an audience—that will develop fluency: automaticity in word recognition, prosody in interpretation, and comprehension in the meaningful performance. Moreover, when students are motivated to perform, you can see their motivation for reading increase by leaps and bounds. Certainly, many of you reading this chapter can remember experiences from your own life when you were motivated to practice by the knowledge that you would eventually be asked to perform—and perhaps become a star!

Points to Ponder

1. If you could design a weekly grand performance for your own classroom, what are some of the steps you would need to take to prepare? Would you include other classes?

2. What are some of the logistical considerations involved in developing your grand performance?

3. How would you make sure that all the students are involved in the grand performance?

4. How might you involve parents and other members of the community in your grand performance?

5. How could you use your grand performance as an opportunity to develop comprehension, vocabulary, and knowledge in other content areas?

Chapter 8: Assessing Fluency

Assessment. Many teachers have a negative association with this word, especially as assessment has become inextricably tied to hurtful comparisons, budget cuts, and worst of all, shame and anxiety in our students. But, perhaps there is a way to look at assessment positively, going back to a more interactive relationship with our data.

Assessment can be categorized by a number of different descriptors. Two major categories that are often used to differentiate approaches to assessment are *summative* and *formative* assessment. Summative assessment is used primarily for making major yes-or-no decisions. Is this school or this classroom meeting learning objectives? Are students in our school system meeting performance goals for reading achievement? The high stakes reading and other academic tests that are given to students each year by various states and the federal government in the United States can be considered summative assessments. Although they can be used to determine whether students, schools, or school systems are meeting certain goals in reading (and if they are not meeting those goals then changes may need to be made), summative assessments do little to impact or improve the day-to-day teaching and learning that goes on inside individual schools, classrooms, and between teachers and individual students.

Fluency is typically not assessed directly in summative assessments. But there are some interesting indicators of a student's future success when we look closely at his or her fluency. One year, I conducted my very own analysis of my students' reading rates as measured with the simple one-minute read and compared them to the two-and-a-half hour reading comprehension test the state required. I put all of the students' scores in order from the most slow and plodding reader to the most proficient reader as indicated by their word-correct-per-minute (WCPM) scores. Then, I put all of the students in order from the lowest state assessment score to the highest state assessment score. The correlation between reading efficiency (fluency and word recognition automaticity) and comprehension was quite evident.

Formative Assessments

Formative assessment, as the name implies, is used to form or shape instruction. Teachers can use the results to determine how much individual students and classrooms are progressing and what kind of changes need to be made if students or classrooms of students are not making appropriate progress.

Formative assessment is mostly a combination of formalized assessment procedures (assessments that are administered, scored, and interpreted in standard ways) and informal assessments and observations (non-standardized assessment procedures in which teachers use their power of observation and their knowledge of reading to make informed decisions on student progress and directions for instruction).

For our purpose, we will focus on formative assessment in fluency and discuss two types of formative assessments—progress monitoring assessment and diagnostic assessment.

Progress Monitoring

As the name suggests, progress monitoring is used to determine whether students are making appropriate progress in reading (in our case, reading fluency) over the course of a school year. Initial assessment starts at the beginning of the school year when teachers determine a baseline of reading achievement in reading fluency. Then, periodically throughout the school year (usually every four to six weeks), students are assessed again using similar procedures in order to determine whether progress is being made, or—using more contemporary terms—to determine whether students are responding to instruction and intervention.

In earlier chapters, we defined the key components of fluency instruction as accuracy in word recognition, automaticity in word recognition, and prosody or expressiveness in oral reading. All three of these elements can be assessed by having students read a reading passage, usually written at the assigned grade level (norms for interpreting this type of assessment are based on students reading a grade-level passage). This type of informal assessment goes by the name of Curriculum Based Assessment (CBA) as students may be asked to read passages that come directly from their reading curriculum.

Passages for a CBA can be taken from students' grade level reading materials. They can also be taken from informal reading inventories (IRIs), which are informal reading assessments made up of graded reading passages that students are asked to read.

The procedure for a CBA is relatively simple. Students are asked to read one or more short grade-level passages orally in their best voice. Following each reading, students may be asked to answer comprehension questions over the reading or give a retelling of the passage. While students read, the teacher or person administering the CBA marks any uncorrected word recognition errors made by the student, marks where the student is after one minute of reading, and attends to the oral expressiveness of the reading. (It should seem clear that, given the complexity of the task for the person administering the CBA, it is a good idea to record each student's reading for later analysis.)

From each reading, the following data can be obtained:

- Word recognition accuracy: Percentage of words read correctly

- Word recognition automaticity: Words read correctly in the first minute

- Oral prosody or expressiveness in reading: The quality of reading as measured against descriptive rubrics

For word recognition accuracy, we are looking for a score of 92–98 percent on grade-level passages. This is indicative of instructional level. Students whose word recognition accuracy is between 92 and 98 percent are right where they should be for their grade level. Scores below 92 percent may indicate problems in word recognition that may need to be addressed. Scores above 98 percent indicate strength or independence in word recognition for that particular student.

Word recognition automaticity is assessed by comparing students' reading rates (words correct per minute, or WCPM) to grade level and time of year norms. Hasbrouck and Tindal (2006) noted that national norms were first established in 1992 following the publication of the National Reading Panel report. Figure 8.1 on the following page shows the 50th percentile norms for grades one through eight based on national oral reading fluency norms from 2005 (Hasbrouck and Tindal 2006). Our goal should be to have students reading at or above the 50th percentile rate by spring for their assigned grade level. Scores significantly below the 50th percentile indicate that automaticity in word recognition may be a concern.

Figure 8.1 National Oral Reading Fluency Norms from 2005

Grade	Percentile	Fall WCPM	Winter WCPM	Spring WCPM
1	90		81	111
	75		47	82
	50		23	53
	25		12	28
	10		6	15
2	90	106	125	142
	75	79	100	117
	50	51	72	89
	25	25	42	61
	10	11	18	31
3	90	128	146	162
	75	90	120	137
	50	71	92	107
	25	44	62	78
	10	21	36	48
4	90	145	166	180
	75	119	139	152
	50	94	112	123
	25	68	87	98
	10	45	61	72
5	90	166	182	194
	75	139	156	18
	50	110	127	139
	25	85	99	109
	10	61	74	83
6	90	177	195	204
	75	153	167	177
	50	127	140	150
	25	98	111	122
	10	68	82	93
7	90	180	192	202
	75	156	165	177
	50	158	136	150
	25	102	109	123
	10	79	88	98
8	90	185	199	199
	75	161	173	177
	50	133	146	151
	25	106	115	124
	10	77	84	97

We should note at this point that, although we have a goal of having our students read at a certain rate by the end of the school year, we do not get students to achieve that goal through emphasis on speed reading. Remember that reading rate is only an indicator of automaticity. We achieve automaticity (which increases in reading rate) in our students by having students read widely and repeatedly for authentic purposes. Reading to increase reading rate is *not* an authentic purpose for reading. Recall that in the previous chapters, we described how automaticity *can* be achieved through authentic practice followed by performance.

Prosody is assessed formatively by listening to students read grade-level passages orally in their best voices and then rating their reading according to a descriptive rubric. Figure 8.2 on the following page represents a rubric that will give you a way to parse out various aspects of prosody in students' reading. After listening to students read, you would rate them for expression and volume in their reading, appropriate phrasing, smoothness versus choppiness, and appropriate pacing (not overall reading rate, but pacing that fits the context of the passage). An overall score of 10 or more indicates that the student is making good progress in fluency. An overall score below 10 indicates that the student needs additional instruction in fluency. By the end of the school year, your goal should be to have students scoring 10 or above on grade-level passages. Scores below 10 may indicate that prosody is a concern for students.

Figure 8.2 Prosody Rubric

	1	2	3	4
Expression and volume	Reads in a quiet voice as if to get words out. The reading does not sound natural like talking to a friend.	Reads in a quiet voice. The reading sounds natural in part of the text, but the reader does not always sound like he or she is talking to a friend.	Reads with volume and expression. However, sometimes the reader slips into expressionless reading and does not sound like he or she is talking to a friend.	Reads with varied volume and expression. The reader sounds like he or she is talking to a friend with his or her voice matching the interpretation of the passage.
Phrasing	Reads word by word in a monotone voice.	Reads in two- or three-word phrases, not adhering to punctuation, stress, and intonation.	Reads with a mixture of run-ons, mid-sentence pauses for breath, and some choppiness. There is reasonable stress and intonation.	Reads with good phrasing, adhering to punctuation, stress, and intonation.
Smoothness	Frequently hesitates while reading, sounds out words, and repeats words or phrases. The reader makes multiple attempts to read the same passage.	Reads with extended pauses or hesitations. The reader has many "rough spots."	Reads with occasional breaks in rhythm. The reader has difficulty with specific words and/or sentence structures.	Reads smoothly with some breaks, but self-corrects with difficult words and/or sentence structures.
Pace	Reads slowly and laboriously.	Reads moderately slowly.	Reads fast and slow throughout reading.	Reads at a conversational pace throughout the reading.

Score _____

Adapted and expanded from Zutell and Rasinski (1991).

Performance Assessments

Earlier in this book, we discussed how having students perform after engaging in a set of practiced readings (rehearsal) is a key for building fluency in authentic and engaging ways. Those performances can themselves be assessed in order to give students and teachers an indication of how students are improving in their actual performances. Figure 8.3 below shows a chart for assessing student performances. (The term *prosody* refers to variation in stress, pitch, and rhythm of speech by which different shades of meaning are conveyed.)

Figure 8.3 Assessment of Student Performances

	Performance	Script	Articulation/ Pronunciation	Prosody/ Expression	Flow Rate	Volume	Total
Student Name	6 pts.	0.5 pts.	0.5 pts.	2 pts.	0.5 pts.	0.5 pts.	10 pts.

On performance days, students will learn more about their own fluency development if they are asked to evaluate themselves and their classmates in a formative manner. It is important that they are familiar with a rubric stating the qualities of fluent reading, guiding them to give articulate responses instead of "it was good" or "it was nice." Ray Reutzel and Robert Cooter (2006) have a wonderful rubric where each characteristic of fluency is shown with a smile or frown (see Figure 8.4 below). I have modified it a bit, and it could be designed differently for various grade levels. By posting a user-friendly fluency rubric in the classroom, the students are constantly reminded what a fluent reader sounds like and they are participating in monitoring their own oral reading development.

Figure 8.4 Are You a Fluent Reader? Rubric

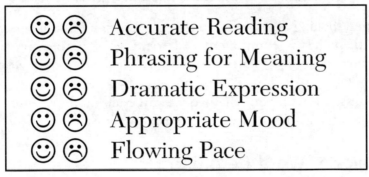

Diagnostic Assessments

In progress-monitoring assessment, the goal is to determine where students are in their reading development and if they are making adequate and appropriate progress. Some students, unfortunately, do not make the kind of progress we would like or expect. If after attempting changes in instruction results in no improvement in student progress, it may be necessary to take a closer look at the student's reading to determine the major concerns that are keeping him or her from progressing. This deeper assessment that aims to identify concerns and strengths is called *diagnostic assessment*. Diagnostic assessment can be done using formal, standardized tests. We feel, however, that more informal diagnostic assessments allow the teacher to control the assessment process and involve the student more closely in identifying those important strengths and concerns. In this section, we present an approach to diagnosis that we call *diagnostic screening*. Diagnostic screening is an informal and quick approach to diagnosis. Instructional time is always limited. And, time given to assessment and diagnosis is time taken from instruction. So, in our diagnostic screening approach, we describe quick, teacher-directed, and curriculum-based approaches to diagnosis that gives teachers a brief but valid assessment of students' strengths and weaknesses in reading. When concerns are identified through the screening process, more intense and deeper diagnostic procedures can be employed, if necessary, to fully understand the nature of the student's problem in reading.

When looking at a student diagnostically, we build assessment around the key components of reading—phonics or word decoding, reading fluency, vocabulary or word meaning, and comprehension. There are many ways to assess each of these. We will share with you what we feel are valid and efficient ways to make diagnostic assessments of students in reading.

Phonics or Word Decoding

A student's ability to decode or "sound out" words can easily be assessed by having that student read graded passages orally and determine the percentage of words read correctly. Scores of 99–100 percent indicate independent reading for the grade level at which the passage is read. A score between 92 and 98 percent generally indicates instructional level, and scores at 91 percent or below indicate frustration level, a level that indicates that the student is having severe difficulty in decoding the words at the grade level that the passage is written.

In other words, if you are working with a fifth-grade student who reads a third-grade passage with 88 percent accuracy, it is clear that the student is at a frustration level in word decoding for grade three materials and above. Word decoding is a major concern and it is likely to have a negative impact on comprehension.

Once you have identified if word decoding is a problem, you can take an even closer qualitative look at the errors the student makes. Do the errors fall in the beginning, middle, or ending parts of words? Do the errors disrupt the meaning of the passage? Do the errors tend to focus on a few features of words, such as certain word families, long vowels, consonant blends, multisyllabic words? Finding a consistent pattern of error will give you direction in developing instruction to meet the needs of the student.

Reading Fluency

As we presented earlier, fluency—the ability to read the words in text automatically and with meaningful expression—is assessed by examining students' reading rate and measuring students' use of prosody in oral reading on grade-level materials. In a diagnostic situation, you would simply ask students to read other materials, some at grade level, and some at grade levels below their assigned placement in order to determine just how far below grade level their fluency problems begin. A fifth grader who also demonstrates problems in fluency with materials written at grade four has a serious concern with fluency that needs to be addressed. Although the student may be able to read the words in those passages correctly, the lack of automaticity and prosody suggest that the student has yet to develop the efficiency in text processing that is manifested in fluency. A more intensive form of the fluency instruction that we have described earlier in this book (e.g., The Fluency Development Lesson) may be appropriate for students demonstrating problems in fluency.

Vocabulary

Vocabulary refers to students' knowledge of the meaning of words in text. Although students may be able to decode words accurately, automatically, and with appropriate expression, if they don't have a solid understanding of the meaning of the words, it is very likely that they will encounter comprehension problems in their reading. Words that are decoded accurately but without knowledge of their meanings are essentially nonsense words.

Vocabulary can easily be assessed in an informal setting. Simply choose 10–20 words that you feel are grade appropriate from a passage that is at your student's assigned grade level. Write the words on a card or sheet of paper. Present the words to your student by showing him or her the word, saying the word aloud, and then asking the student to provide you with a definition, a sentence that illustrates the meaning, or some other form of evidence that he or she may know the meaning of the word (e.g., draw a picture or display an action of whatever the word may represent). You may ask your student to elaborate on his or her definition if you feel he or she has not provided a sufficiently detailed explanation.

You can give full credit (10 points), half credit (five points), or no credit for each word depending on the nature and sufficiency of their explanations. Then, determine the percentage score for each student. If a student received full credit for six words, half credit for two words, and no credit for two words, his or her score would be 70 percent ([6 x 10] + [2 x 5] + [2 x 0] = 70). Scores should then be interpreted in the following manner:

$\geq 90\%$	=	independent level
60%–80%	=	instructional level
$\leq 50\%$	=	frustration level

The results from the student above indicate that his or her vocabulary appears to be at a level appropriate for his or her grade placement for instruction. Vocabulary levels identified at the frustration level would give us cause to look more deeply into a student's vocabulary to determine, perhaps using an instrument such as the Peabody Picture Vocabulary Test (Dunn and Dunn 2007), a more detailed assessment of his or her vocabulary.

Comprehension

Comprehension, of course, is the essential goal of reading, the ability to make meaning from a passage that is read. Comprehension can be tricky to assess and diagnose because comprehension problems can be caused by difficulties in word decoding and fluency, among other factors.

In order to overcome the confounding effects of word decoding and fluency, we suggest the following screening approach for comprehension:

- Present the student with a brief (100- to 300-word passage) written at his or her assigned grade level.

- Have the student follow along silently while you read the passage to the student (this removes the problems in decoding and fluency that may impact comprehension).

- Once the passage has been read, remove the passage from the student and ask him or her to retell or summarize what he or she has read. Feel free to prompt the student if you feel that an incomplete retelling has been given.

- Rate the students' retelling using the rubric shown in Figure 8.5 on the following page. Use your best professional judgment to make your rating. Make notes on the student's retelling.

- If you require confirmation of your initial rating, repeat the process using other passages or passages written at grade levels below or above the student's placement.

- Ratings or scores of one or two are indicative of inadequate (frustration level) comprehension processing for the grade-level of the passage read. Frustration level comprehension for grade level passages suggest a diagnosis of comprehension processing as a major concern for the student.

Figure 8.5 Comprehension Rubric (Rasinski and Padak 2007)

Frustration Level

1 No recall or minimal recall of only a fact or two from the passage.

2 Student recalls a number of unrelated facts of varied importance in no logical order.

Instructional Level

3 Student recalls the main idea of the passage with a few supporting details, in a generally logical order.

4 Student recalls the main idea along with a fairly robust set of supporting details, although not necessarily organized logically or sequentially as presented in the passage.

Independent Level

5 Student recall is a comprehensive summary of the passage, presented in a logical order and/or with a robust set of details, and includes a statement of main idea.

6 Student makes reasonable connections beyond the text to his or her own personal life, another text, etc.

Conclusion

Assessment and diagnosis are integral parts of instruction. Unless we can determine the current level of reading performance for our students, determine whether our instructional efforts are making a difference in our students' reading, and determine areas of concern for students with reading problems, we are essentially teaching in the dark. We won't know if our students are making progress or what we need to focus on if our students are experiencing problems in reading.

In this chapter, we present simple, quick, teacher-directed, and valid approaches to assessment and diagnosis. We recognize that these approaches are only a first step in understanding our students, their progress in reading, and any challenges that they may face in making adequate progress. For a deeper understanding and analysis of some students, a deeper assessment is necessary. That deeper understanding is beyond the scope of this book. However, with what we have presented, you have the tools necessary for making your fluency and general reading instruction more effective—by being able to determine if students are responding appropriately to our instruction. If our assessments indicate that students are responding well, then we know to keep doing what we are doing—it's working! However, if our assessments indicate that students' response to our instruction is not adequate, then we know that we need to do something different—provide differential instruction that meets their needs. That is what good instruction is all about.

Points to Ponder

1. What is the purpose of assessment in your own classroom? How do you use the results of assessment?

2. What are some of the problems that you see with assessment?

3. How does the approach to assessment and diagnosis fit with your own conception of assessment? What changes would you have to make in order for this approach to work in your classroom?

4. How do the assessments already required or available in your school fit with the formative assessments described here in the areas of phonics, fluency, vocabulary, and comprehension?

Chapter 9: Looking Behind Us, Looking Ahead

"This is what you shall do: Love the earth and sun and the animals, despise riches, give alms to everyone that asks, stand up for the stupid and crazy, devote your income and labor to others, hate tyrants, argue not concerning God, have patience and indulgence toward the people, take off your hat to nothing known or unknown, or to any man or number of men, go freely with powerful uneducated persons, and with the young and with the mothers of families...re-examine all you have been told in school or church or in any book, dismiss whatever insults your own soul; and your very flesh shall be a great poem and have the richest fluency not only in its words but in the silent lines of its lips and face and between the lashes of your eyes and in every motion and joint of your body."

Walt Whitman
Preface to Leaves of Grass *(1855)*

We begin this chapter with this famous preface by Walt Whitman for a number of reasons. First, his directives to "...Love the earth and sun and the animals,...have patience and indulgence toward the people,...go freely with powerful uneducated persons, and with the young and with the mothers of families...re-examine all you have been told...", in essence captures the role of a teacher—to embrace the world, to work with the uneducated, to help others think critically. Second, he uses the term *fluency* to describe the fullness of life that is the goal of every teacher for his or her students. And third, he tells us that our lives can become a poem, a text meant to be expressed orally and meant to move others deeply. For life to become a poem, however, we need to experience, read, and perform poems. And performing poems means that we need to practice.

We read poetry ourselves for pleasure. And, we know poems are meant to be practiced and performed. We also have learned that, through repeated oral practice, we come to deeper understandings of what the poet means to convey through his or her poem. Poetry leads to practice, which leads to performance, and culminates in comprehension.

Where We Have Been

In this book, we have tried to make several key points:

- Reading fluency is critical to students' success in learning to read.

- Practice, both wide and repeated or deep, is key to developing fluency.

- Oral performance of a reading passage gives students an authentic motivation to engage in reading practice (rehearsal).

- Certain texts lend themselves to oral (prosodic) performance. These are texts that are written with a sense of voice and include reader's theater scripts, dialogues, monologues, poetry, songs, oratory, letters, diaries, and journals.

When students know that they will be performing a dramatic interpretation of a reader's theater script or poem, they know that they will have to practice or rehearse in order to give a performance that an audience will find satisfying and in which the students themselves can take pride. Students love doing this sort of fluency work. And, we know that it works—not only in developing fluency, but also in improving students' overall reading achievement and motivation for reading.

Both practice and performance are integral parts of the Kent State University reading clinic (directed by Tim Rasinski). Students regularly are assigned a poem, script, song, or other text that they rehearse in school and at home. Indeed, the final day of each semester is marked by a grand performance in which students perform for their parents, grandparents, and others the material that they had been working on throughout the weeks of the clinic. The students beam with delight as they perform for their audience and receive the justifiable praise of their teachers and family members.

The children who participate in the reading clinic are struggling readers who are not simply well behind in their reading development, but who also tend to find reading an onerous task. The authentic practice and performance in which students engage becomes a transformative experience as students see that they can master texts, that they can read with expression and meaning, and that they can find reading a fun and enjoyable activity. Most students who participate in the reading clinic, normally about a month in duration, will make significantly more than a month's progress in reading. We have seen many students make as much as one to two years' progress!

But practice and performance is also an integral part of the reading clinic that takes place in a fifth grade classroom. Each week, students rehearse a text that is assigned on Monday and performed at the end of the week. Students make remarkable gains in reading achievement and confidence in themselves as readers. Struggling readers in Lorraine's classroom have made on average 2.9 years' growth in reading achievement in the one year they are in her classroom (Griffith and Rasinski 2004). Moreover, they made more than double the gain in reading fluency (as measured by reading rate) than what would normally be expected of fifth graders—even though she knew the goal of her fluency program was never for her students to read fast or faster.

Chase Young, a second-grade teacher in McKinney, Texas, reports that his students made exceptional growth in reading comprehension and reading achievement when he introduced practice and performance into his classroom (Young and Rasinski 2009). Dana Solomon, a fifth-grade teacher from Frisco, Texas, found that her class, on average, had the highest scores in reading on the state mandated reading achievement test after making practice and performance a central part of her reading curriculum. And Rhonda Powell from South Carolina reported to us significant improvements in her high- and low-achieving readers through the implementation of practice and performance. We could go on and on with studies and testimonials. However, we think the point is made. Practice and performance in reading, when done in the way that we describe in this book, is good pedagogy. Practice and performance is not just fun; it's good, solid, and effective teaching of reading.

Teaching Reading— an Art and a Science

Over the past decade, the teaching of reading has been approached as a science. Researchers have been reporting on scientific findings that teachers have been required to implement in their instruction. While, in general, treating reading as a science is positive and has resulted in significant improvements in reading achievement, it has also had some unintended consequences. The art of teaching has been taken out of the reading classroom. Reading is viewed more as a skill to be mastered rather than an activity of the mind that is to be embraced, enjoyed, and appreciated. The scientific approach to reading has led to some odd manifestations of reading instruction—good reading has become fast reading; reading instruction has become dominated by assessments in which teachers and students chart their progress; reading instruction has tended to be marked primarily by informational texts, stories, and decodable texts—no time for authentic poetry, plays, songs, and other texts that are simply fun to read and perform. And there is never enough time for students to live in the words of a famous writer, orator, and leader who challenged and changed the culture in which we live—like Frederick Douglass or Sojourner Truth.

Teaching reading is not just a science, it is an art. Teachers' classrooms are their canvases. It is not enough to teach students the skill of reading; they need to have the aesthetic experience of reading a text that brings a person to tears or performing a script or poem that leaves an audience speechless. Reading needs to be an enjoyable and satisfying experience for students—otherwise, we may teach students to read, but they may find reading such an unrewarding experience that they will choose not to read when they have a chance. As Mark Twain is credited with saying, "Those who choose not to read have no advantage over those who can't read." The teaching of reading, when approached as an art, focuses on developing in students a love for reading, a love for the written and well-chosen word.

This is what we have tried to share with you in this book—teaching is an art and one way to embrace the artistic component of reading is to have students engage in authentic performances of texts, as well as the dedicated practice that precedes any worthwhile performance. The science of reading has found that, when students engage in practice and performance of this sort, they will also make remarkable improvements in the skill of reading.

Many of you reading this book can look back at your own experiences in school and home and recall times when you practiced reading something in anticipation of performing it for an audience. That audience may have been your grandparents or your classmates, but it was still an audience. We bet that for most of you this is a fond memory that you will cherish for the rest of your lives. What you may not know is that same experience, which you did mostly for the fun of doing it, also helped you become the good reader that you are today.

We do not see students in schools today having the same opportunities to perform scripts, poems, songs, and other texts for audiences. The science of teaching reading has focused teachers' and students' attention on only those instructional activities that have been proven, through science, to improve reading achievement. Performance-type activities are not viewed as scientifically based; rather, they are seen as fluff, activities that can be done only when the "real" work of reading instruction is completed.

We are here to tell you that performance and its accompanying practice should be the work of reading instruction. Certainly, it embraces the artistic side of reading and reading instruction, but the theory and the ever-growing research based on practice and performance tells us that this is also scientifically based—it is science.

The art and science of teaching reading need not be mutually exclusive. The best teachers we know are both artists and scientists. If you are interested in bringing the art and science of teaching reading together into your classroom, we hope you will consider dedicating daily instructional time for authentic practice and performance of texts that are meant to be practiced and performed—scripts, poems, songs, and the like. For some of you it will be affirming—affirming what you already do or what you have done in the past but stopped when you were told that only scientifically based instruction can occur in your classroom. For some of you, it will be enlightening—perhaps you might be saying to yourself, "I never thought about reading instruction in this way before." For all of you and your students, we hope (and know) that it will be transformative. It will transform your classroom where reading is no longer only a scientific skill to be mastered, but also an art to be appreciated and enjoyed for its aesthetic value. Perhaps, paraphrasing Whitman, you and your students and your classroom can "become a great poem filled with the richest form of fluency."

We thank you for reading this volume and we leave you with one final poem. It is our wish for you for the future as you embark on this new artistic and poetic approach to fluency instruction. We wish you success. And we think that the following poem (whose origin is disputed but sometimes attributed to the American philosopher Ralph Waldo Emerson), with the postscript added by us, captures what it means to be successful in life:

To laugh often and love much; to win the respect of intelligent persons and the affection of children; to earn the approbation of honest citizens and endure the betrayal of false friends; to appreciate beauty; to find the best in others; to give of one's self; to leave the world a bit better, whether by a healthy child, a garden patch, or a redeemed social condition; to have played and laughed with enthusiasm and sung with exultation; to know even one life has breathed easier because you have lived—this is to have succeeded.

And, we could add, this is to have been a teacher!

Points to Ponder

1. Comprehension is the ultimate goal of reading instruction. Does comprehension occur during the practice and become evident in the performance, or does it occur after students have performed the text in a meaningful way?

2. How do you think meaning is made during reading?

Allington, R. L. 1983. Fluency: The neglected goal of the reading program. *The Reading Teacher*, 36:556–561.

Carbo, M. 1978a. Teaching reading with talking books. *The Reading Teacher*, 32:267–273.

———(1978b). A word imprinting technique for children with severe memory disorders. *Teaching exceptional children*, 11:3–5.

Cassidy, J. and D. Cassidy. 2009. What's hot for 2009. *Reading Today*, 26(4):1, 8, 9.

Chomsky, C. 1976. After decoding: What? *Language Arts*, 53:288–296.

Daane, M. C., J. R. Campbell, W. S. Grigg, M. J. Goodman, and A. Oranje. 2005. *Fourth-grade students reading aloud: NAEP 2002 special study of oral reading*. Washington, D.C.: U.S. Department of Education, Institute of Education Sciences.

Dowhower, S. L. 1991. Speaking of prosody: Fluency's unattended bedfellow. *Theory into Practice*, 30:165–175.

Duke, N. K., M. Pressley, and K. Hilden. 2004. Difficulties in reading comprehension. In C. A. Stone, E. R. Silliman, B. J. Ehren, and K. Apel. 2004. *Handbook of language and literacy: Development and disorders*. New York: The Guilford Press.

Dunn, L. M. and D. Dunn. 2007. Peabody Picture Vocabulary Test. 2004. 4th ed. San Antonio, TX: Pearson Educaton, Inc.

Gamse, B. C., H. S. Bloom, J. J. Kemple, R. T. Jacob, B. Boulay, L. Bozzi, L. Caswell, M. Horst, W. C. Smith, R. G. St. Pierre, and F. Unlu. 2008. Reading First impact study: Interim report. Washington, D.C.: U.S. Department of Education.

Griffith, L. and T. Rasinski. 2004. A focus on fluency: How one teacher incorporated fluency with her reading curriculum. *The Reading Teacher*, 58 (2), 126–137.

Hasbrouck, J. and G. Tindal. 2006. Oral reading fluency norms: A valuable assessment tool for reading teachers. *The Reading Teacher*. April. 59(7):636–644.

Martinez, M., N. Roser, and S. Strecker. 1999. I never thought I could be a star: A reader's theater ticket to reading fluency. *The Reading Teacher*, 52:326–334.

National Reading Panel. 2000. *Report of the National Reading Panel: Teaching children to read. Report of the subgroups.* Washington, D.C.: U.S. Department of Health and Human Services, National Institutes of Health.

Pearson, P. D. and M. C. Gallagher. 1983. The instruction of reading comprehension. *Contemporary Educational Psychology*. 8:317–344.

Pinnell, G. S., J. J. Pikulski, K. K. Wixson, J. R. Campbell, P. B. Gough, and A. S. Beatty. 1995. Listening to children read aloud. Washington, D.C.: U.S. Department of Education, Office of Educational Research and Improvement.

Pluck, M. 1995. Rainbow Reading programme: Using taped stories. *Reading Forum*, 1, 25–29.

Rasinski, T. V. 2003. *The fluent reader: Oral reading strategies for building word recognition, fluency, and comprehension.* New York: Scholastic.

Rasinski, T. V. and J. V. Hoffman. 2003. Theory and research into practice: Oral reading in the school literacy curriculum. *Reading Research Quarterly*, 38:510–522.

Rasinski, T. V. and N. Padak. 2007. *Three minute reading assessments*. New York: Scholastic.

Rasinski, T. V. and N. Padak, Linek, Sturtevant. 1995. Fast Start: A parental involvement reading program for primary grade students. In *Generations of Literacy. Seventeenth Yearbook of the College Reading Association*, 301-312. Harrisonburg, VA: College Reading Association.

Rasinski, T.V., A. Rikli, and S. Johnston. 2009. Reading fluency: More than automaticity? More than a concern for the primary grades? *Literacy research and instruction*, 48:350-361.

Reutzel, D. R. and R. Cooter. 2006. *Strategies for reading assessment and instruction: Helping every child succeed*, 3rd ed. Upper Saddle River, NJ: Prentice Hall.

Reutzel, D. R., C. D. Jones, P. C. Fawson, and J. A. Smith. 2008. Scaffolded silent reading: A complement to guided repeated oral reading that works! *The Reading Teacher*, 62(3):194–207.

Samuels, S. J. 1979. The method of repeated readings. *The Reading Teacher*, 32:403–408.

Schreiber, P. A. 1987. Prosody and structure in children's syntactic processing. In R. Horowitz and S. J. Samuels (eds.), *Comprehending oral and written language*, 243–270. New York: Academic Press.

———. 1991. Understanding prosody's role in reading acquisition. *Theory into Practice*, 30:158–164.

Schreiber, P. A., and C. Read. 1980. Children's use of phonetic cues in spelling, parsing, and—maybe—reading. *Bulletin of the Orton Society*, 30:209–224.

Stone, C. A., E. R. Silliman, B. J. Ehren, and K. Apel. 2004. *Handbook of language and literacy: Development and disorders*, 501–520. New York: The Guilford Press.

Therrien, W. J. 2004. Fluency and comprehension gains as a result of repeated reading: A meta-analysis. *Remedial and Special Education*, 25(4):252–261.

Topping, K. 2001. *Thinking reading writing: A practical guide to paired learning with peers, parents & volunteers*. New York and London: Continuum International.

Young, C. and T. Rasinski, T. 2009. Implementing reader's theater as an approach to classroom fluency instruction. *The Reading Teacher*, September. 64(1), 4-13.

Zutell, J. and T. Rasinski. 1991. Training teachers to attend to their students' oral reading fluency. *Theory into Practice*, 30, 211-217.

Abbott, Bud and Lou Costello. Who's on First? Stardust Records. Available at: http://www.audible.com, 2008.

Carroll, Lewis. 1865. *Alice's Adventures in Wonderland*. Norwood, MA: Norwood Press, 2009.

Churchill, Winston. 1940. Blood, Toil, Tears and Sweat. The Churchill Centre and Churchill War Rooms, London. https// www.winstonchurchill.org

Davis, Jefferson. Inaugural Address. American Rhetoric. http:// www.americanrhetoric.com

Dear America Series. 1996-2004. New York: Scholastic, Inc.

Dickens, Charles. 1922. *A Tale of Two Cities*. New York: The MacMillan Company, 1997.

Emmett, Daniel. 1843. Boatman Dance. From *Building Fluency Through Practice & Performance*, Rasinski, Tim and Lorraine Griffith. Huntington Beach, CA: Shell Education, 2008.

Fleischman, Paul. 1989. *I Am Phoenix: Poems for Two Voices*. New York: HarperCollins Children's Books.

Frost, Robert. 1920. The Road Not Taken. *The Road Not Taken and Other Poems*. Dover Publications, 1993.

Gamse, Albert. 1810. Hail to The chief, 1954.

Griffith, Lorraine. A Reader's Theater for Five Voices. West Buncombe Elementary. Asheville, NC.

Hopkins, Lee Bennett. 2009. *My America: A Poetry Atlas of the United States*. New York: Simon & Schuster.

Howitt, Mary. 1829. *The Spider and The Fly*. New York: Harcourt, 2002.

Hughes, Langston. 1932. Alabama Earth. *The Dreamkeepers and Other Poems*. New York: Knopf Books for Young Readers, 1996.

———. 1922. Mother to Son. *Harlem Night Song*. New York: Scholastic, 2009.

Isecke, Harriet. *The Sojourner Truth Story*. Huntington Beach, CA: Teacher Created Materials, 2009.

Lincoln, Abraham. Cooper Union Speech. American Rhetoric. http://www.americanrhetoric.com.

———. First Inaugural Address. American Rhetoric. http://www.americanrhetoric.com.

———. Gettysburg Address. American Rhetoric. http://www.americanrhetoric.com.

———. Second Inaugural Address. American Rhetoric. http://www.americanrhetoric.com.

Lobel, Arnold. *Frog and Toad* box set series. New York: Harper Collins. (1970–1979/2004).

Longfellow, Henry Wadsworth. The Midnight Ride of Paul Revere. *Tales of a Wayside Inn*. Boston: Houghton Mifflin. (1863/1915)

Lord of the Rings: The Motion Picture Trilogy. DVD. Directed by Peter Jackson. New Line Home Entertainment, 2004.

McRae, John. 1915. In Flanders Fields. *In Flanders Fields: And Other Poems of the First World War*. Busby, B. (Ed.) London: Arcturus Publishing, Ltd., 2008.

Rasinski, Tim. *Daily Word Ladders*. New York: Scholastic, 2005.

Rasinski, Tim and Lorraine Griffith. *Building Fluency Through Practice & Performance: American History*. Huntington Beach, CA: Shell Education, 2007.

————. *Texts for Fluency Practice, Level C*. Huntington Beach, CA: Shell Education, 2005.

Rasinski, Tim, Lorraine Griffith, and Stephen Griffith. SingReadLearn. Available at: http://www.singreadlearn.com.

Rasinski, Tim and Roger Heym. *Making and Writing Words*. Huntington Beach, CA: Shell Education, 2007.

Steig, William. 1982. *Dr. DeSoto*. New York: Farrar, Straus, and Giroux, 1990.

————. 1988. *Sylvester and The Magic Pebble*. New York: Simon & Shuster, 2009.

Sterling, Andrew and Kerry Mills. Meet Me in St. Louis, Louis, Sydney: J. Albert & Son, 1904.

Sullivan Ballou Letter. PBS.org. http://www.pbs.org/civilwar/war/ballou_letter.html.

Whitman, Walt. 1855. Preface to Leaves of Grass. *Whitman Poetry and Prose*. New York: Penguin, 1996.

Notes